FAITH &
COURAGE

Overcoming the FEAR that keeps you from
FRUITFULNESS

---

david j. drum

DEDICATION

To the saints at The Potter's House Christian Fellowship Church in Meadowlands, SOWETO, South Africa.

CONTENTS

FOREWORD

INTRODUCTION

PART 1 - FEAR   1

PART 2 - COURAGE   20

PART 3 - FAITH   44

PART 4 - FRUITFULNESS 67

APPENDIX   92

NOTES   95

ABOUT THE AUTHOR 99

FOREWORD

Life has to be about more than just you. No one will succeed without building your life around something larger than yourself. We all long for purpose and meaning in life and this can never be satisfied when we live only for selfish ambition. *[Philippians 2:4] "Let each of you look out not only for his own interests, but also for the interests of others."*

[Colossians 3:2] "Set your mind on things above, not on things on the earth." This, in part, spells out the clear mandate of the Gospel for each of us; *THERE IS A DIMENSION BEYOND SELF INTEREST THAT MUST CAPTIVATE OUR LIVES.*

This was the center piece of Jesus' appeal to the disciples. Every time self became the focus, their small mindedness was met with a rebuke. They were caught by Jesus arguing among themselves, *[Luke 22:24] "Now there was also a dispute among them, as to which of them should be considered the greatest."* This was, of course, the wrong approach. Jesus responded by saying; *[Luke 22:26] "But not so among you; on the contrary, he who is greatest among you, let him be as the younger, and he who governs as he who serves."* His word to them is His word to us...*GET YOUR EYES OFF OF YOURSELF.* This is what is required, even demanded by Jesus for each of us. The Great Commission: *"Go into all the world and preach the Gospel to all creation",* requires a heart fixated on a life poured out in service for others.

Now, you may be asking at this point, what does all this have to do with the title of this book, *Faith and Courage; Overcoming the Fear That Keeps You from Fruitfulness?* Here is my point: Life is a great adventure and the adventure only begins when you respond to God's call for your life. However that may express itself in each individual, *IT IS A CALL TO FRUITFULNESS. [John 15:16] "You did not choose Me, but I chose you and appointed you that you should go and bear fruit, and that your fruit should remain, that whatever you ask the Father in My name He may give you."*

This call to fruitfulness will thrust you into an arena where you have never been and where you may think you are not prepared. The Gospel is never about playing it safe but about challenging your life in ways that have never been challenged. Once you cross the threshold to live beyond your own interests and serve God for the purpose of bearing fruit you will encounter the unknown. The disciples did not know what they were in for when Jesus called them to preach the Gospel in all the world. *THEY WERE GOING TO NEED THE HIGHEST LEVELS OF FAITH AND COURAGE IN ORDER TO OVERCOME THE OBSTACLES THEY WERE GOING TO FACE IN ORDER TO BE FRUITFUL.*

Whatever God has for your life, the same will be true. A life of faith is all about challenge and risk. You will never experience all that God has for you as long as you play it safe and maintain the status quo of doing only what you feel comfortable with. Your personal *'comfort zone'* is an enemy of God's will for your life. A comfort zone is constructed in such a way that we avoid any situation that we are fearful of or where we find we don't have the courage to step out. *OVERCOMING YOUR FEAR WILL BE ONE OF THE GREATEST VICTORIES IN YOUR LIFE....IT IS WHAT IS KEEPING YOU FROM GOD'S BEST.* If there is ever a time when courage is needed by the people of God it is **NOW!** Courage is liberating. Courage will empower you to advance against the giants that you are called to confront in your life. The story of David and Goliath is a good example of this. All the components are there: An obstacle that is intimidating that causes us to cower in fear and refuse to move forward; an army of trained, fighting men is reduced to being immobilized by one giant; a giant that insists that you fight on his terms. *DAVID REFUSED,* as you must refuse. The army of Israel is fearful, but David is filled with faith and courage. Who would you rather be like? Who wins ultimately? Of course, we know the answer.

This book can be a great tool and instrument in the hands of God to assist you in your life to overcome and discover the fruitfulness that God has called you to achieve. Pray over its challenge for your life. God has great things for each of us, your challenge is to discover God's will for your life and acquire the faith and courage to obey Him and carry it out. By the time you finish this book, may God have helped you get closer to the life of fruitfulness that He has for you.

Paul Stephens,
El Paso, TX

INTRODUCTION

You might have heard the story of a hitchhiker on a country road. Not a lot of cars go by on a country road, so you take what you can get. An old rickety flat bed truck comes along with worn wood out railing around the bed. The grateful hitcher hops into the back of the truck and is shocked that the cargo he is to share space with is a beautifully polished black casket with gold handles. As the truck rides down the road, our hitchhiking friend admires the craftsmanship of the casket and the creator's attention to detail for something that is only going to be buried in the ground. Then it starts to rain. The casket is now his only shelter. After making sure it is empty, he crawls in to get out of the rain. The inside was plush with white silk lining and padding on every side. The hum of the road and the complete darkness all add up to the comfy coffin being the perfect napping spot.

After a sufficient snooze, our friend awakes from the dead, so to speak. Remembering where he is after several moments, he opens the lid slightly to see the outside conditions. Two more hitchhikers have been picked up in the mean time and he sees them sitting there leaning against the truck railing. Without thinking of how this would be perceived, the awakened man opens the lid a little more, sticks his head out and asks, "Hey, is it still raining?" Terror immediately grips the unsuspecting passengers. They both yell a blood-curdling scream and escape by jumping out of the back of the truck, while it is moving sixty miles per hour down the road, sustaining bodily injury.

Fear will cause you to make bad decisions!

Sometimes the worst decision is doing nothing. Fear can paralyze you and keep you from doing what you know you should do; what you want to do; have the ability to do, and what God would call you to do.

The problem is not fear itself. Fear is a God given emotion that has its place. Sometimes it is smart to be afraid. The problem is our reaction to fear. The purpose of this book is to teach you to recognize fear and overcome it through courage and faith; to step out regardless of your fears; to refuse to let timidity keep you from your God-given goals, calling, and fruitfulness.

Keep alert. Be firm in your faith. Stay brave and strong.1 Corinthians 16:13 CEV

PART 1 - FEAR

I sought the LORD, and he answered me and delivered me from all my fears. Psalms 34:4 ESV

You are not abnormal for feeling fear. Picking up this book does not make you wimpy (It is what you do about it that counts). Surveys show that many people will admit to having fear and yet very few confess that fear is holding them back from life's adventure. We like to portray the image to others that we are bold and courageous. In truth, insecurity abounds in the majority of people. You are not alone!

God told Gideon his army was too big (Judges 6). If they had won the battle, they would be tempted to think it was by their own strength. God wanted them to know beyond any shadow of doubt it was he who gave them the victory. So, God told Gideon to send home anyone who was afraid. Twenty-two thousand men left! On the outside, they all looked like brave warriors. However, inside they were filled with fear, doubt and insecurity. Fear is a common issue most people deal with.

David and Goliath is one of the most famous of all

Bible stories. People love to support the underdog because we relate so well to him. The context of the story is fear. Goliath has stepped onto the battlefield each day and called out for a man from Israel to fight him. The entire army of Israel is intimidated, hiding behind rocks and behind trees. Admittedly, Goliath is a big guy, but he is only one guy and Israel has an entire army (Not to mention God on their side). It is into this arena that David comes from tending his father's sheep and answers the challenge to face the giant (1 Samuel 17). David seems fearless. We would like to picture ourselves as bold as he was, but most of us can better identify with the intimidated army of Israel.

Fear has torment

We have all experienced being afraid. Perhaps you have heard a noise in the middle of the night. In your half-asleep state of mind, you interpret the sound to be somebody in the house. I mean, "It is the only reasonable explanation." In your mind, you can imagine in which room the intruder is and what he (or it) is doing. Then the "What ifs" begin: murder, rape, arson and other terrible crimes go through your head. What if he is in the children's room? What if he is in your room right now staring at you and wondering if you are awake? He will probably murder you so there will not be any witnesses. And so, you lay there perfectly still, frozen by fear that is made up in your mind.

The Bible tells us that fear has torment (1 John 4:18). Many live their lives immobilized by fear. They will not go out after dark, will not drive at certain times of the day or not at all, they will not use public rest rooms and the list goes on. These things become such a part of the routine that we do not think of it as fear or paranoia. We reason, "This is just the way I was made." However, in reality, we are being held back by fear. The mind is tormented by doubt and worry about kids, crime, economy, people's opinion, bills, etc. We worry about things we cannot control. We worry about things that do not matter. People become prisoners to their fears. They will not let the kids breathe because of fear. Every time the dog barks, "I wonder who is out there." Fear can be irrational.

In an effort to preserve peace of mind, we build bigger and bigger walls around our lives. We install safety nets and security devices. In our personality, we design defense mechanisms to protect ourselves. These are all motivated by fear, worry and doubt. But, it does not purchase peace of mind because the fear is inside of us. We either identify the issue and deal with it, or build bigger walls. If you are afraid of crime, no security system in the world will give you peace. If you are afraid of germs, living in a sterile bubble still will not make that fear go away. The fear of getting hurt by others would continue to torment you even if you lived on a deserted island.

Fear is a tool of the enemy. It brings physical suffering, disease, mental anguish, and distress. In his book Deadly Emotions, Don Colbert, M.D. makes this connection clear: "Fear has been associated with a wide variety of diseases, including cardiovascular diseases and hypertension; digestive-tract diseases such as colitis, Crohn's disease, irritable bowel syndrome, and ulcers; headaches; and skin disorders such as psoriasis, eczema, and stress acne. Fear can cause a decreased immune response, which may lead to frequent infections or the development of deadly disease. Fear can precede a heart attack...or even death." **1.**

The cliché, *scared to death,* comes from real life events. One such account is found in the Bible (1 Samuel 25). A man by the name of Nabal owned many sheep that were lead to grazing areas by shepherds. These herds would wander far from home at times and this made them vulnerable to theft. Fortunately, for Nabal, David and his men were in the area and provided protection. When the time came for the sheep to be gathered home for shearing, David sent a few men to request provision from Nabal for the service he had provided. Nabal refused to acknowledge David's help and rejected the request. David became furious and rallied his men for battle. The name Nabal means *fool*, and he lived up to his name. However, one thing Nabal did have going for him was a wise wife. Abigail heard of what had happened and immediately prepared a gift of food and grain, had her servants load several donkeys, and sent the gift to David without informing her husband. When she met David on the way, she presented the gift and begged for mercy on her husband and her household. The gift was accepted and the whole situation was diffused. She returned home and the next day told her husband how close he had come to being killed. When he heard this, the Bible says, "his heart died within him, and he became like a stone (VS 37)." Fear sent him into cardiac arrest and he died ten days later. He was scared to death!

It has been said that ulcers are not caused by what you eat, but by what is eating you. Stress is the defining element of our generation. Anxiety disorders are the most common mental illness in the United States. Jesus predicted that a sign of the later days would be "men's hearts failing them from fear (Luke 21:26)."

The gift of fear

Is crime real? Of course! I am not suggesting you disconnect your brain. Sometimes it is smart to be afraid. God has given the emotion of fear to protect and preserve us from harm's way. It is a gift. Survival is an instinct that we do not have to give much thought to. When faced with danger, there is a powerful adrenaline rush that enables us to either run away or fight for our life. Fight or flight decisions are made in a nanosecond by the instinct of fear.

We are programmed to know certain boundaries. Other lines not to be crossed, such as touching a hot stove, we learn from experience. Many of these lines should be respected and not ignored. Stop signs are a good example. We are not afraid of stop signs, but we respect them because of what might happen if we ignore them. This is not being bound by fear, this is being practical.

As a child, fear kept me walking the straight and narrow path. This is a good thing! The fear of a belt against my posterior produced many wise decisions. Children who never experience the consequences of bad behavior are shocked when they grow up and real life slaps them in the face.

Fear can be a motivator for good. The lazy person gets up and goes to work for fear of not having food to eat. The husband or wife does not make that large spontaneous purchase for fear of what the spouse might say. The teenager studies for the exam because a bad grade will disqualify them from sports. You get the point. Although this book is about how fear can be distorted, we have to acknowledge fear does have use and benefit.

Perhaps you have heard the story of the rich Texan who had an only child, a beautiful daughter of age to marry. This man owned lots of land with oil wells, crops and many head of cattle. He wanted to make sure his daughter married the right man. One summer evening, he had a coming out party for his daughter and invited all the neighbors, friends, relatives and, of course, all the eligible young men from the area. Behind his mansion, there was an Olympic size pool that he stocked full of alligators for the occasion. He challenged the eager young men who were present to a test: the one who would swim the length of the pool would have three prizes to choose from: 1) five million dollars, 2) ten thousand acres of land with oil wells, or 3) the hand of his daughter in marriage, which would mean inheriting everything. As soon as the words were out of the Texan's mouth, a splash was heard at one end of the pool. Seconds later, a dripping young man emerged from the opposite end. The impressed rancher asked the young man if he wanted the five million dollars as his reward. The young man said, "No!" "Well," the rancher asked, "Do you want the ten thousand acres of land with oil wells?" The young man declined. "So," the rancher asked with a grin, "You want my daughter's hand in marriage?" "No sir!" The rancher was confused, "That was the only three choices. What is it that you want?" The young man looked at the group surrounding them and said, "I'd like to know the name of the dude that pushed me in the pool."

Fear can be something that motivates us for accomplishment.

...through the fear of the LORD a man avoids evil. Proverbs 16:6 NIV

Whom do you serve?

Fear, as with other emotions, can cause us to be anything but practical. We have all had times when we let our emotions drive us. Anger, desire and passion seem to override all reason and logic. When our emotions are erupting, we become vulnerable to exploitation. Marketers are trained to aim at people's emotions and not logic for this very reason. Logically speaking, we would not buy half the things we do. The "have to have it" emotion causes us to give in to the sales pitch. Emotions alone are not a good basis for making decisions. Life would be boring without some feeling for sure, but you cannot go through life controlled by what feels good. The mantra, "How can it be wrong if it feels so right," is unfortunately the operating motto of many in our culture today. In our schools, we are more concerned about hurting feelings than about teaching our children to succeed. Prisons are filled with people guilty of crimes of passion.

Men today are emotional. Somehow this has been elevated to a virtue. If a man is not in touch with his feminine side, he is characterized as a brute. In this atmosphere, it becomes completely acceptable to give into the feeling of fear. We avoid things that make us feel anxious or force us out of our comfort zone. We are servants of our emotions.

Fear is an emotional issue, but it is also a spiritual one. Fear can be an area of our life that becomes a stronghold of the enemy. Fear keeps us from doing what God has called us to do and from having what God has promised. In truth, you will serve whom you fear. If you fear the Lord, you will serve Him. If you fear people's opinion, you will live to please them. Many are serving the wrong things and are in spiritual bondage because of fear. Satan's desire is to hinder you from making progress in your life and one of his favorite tools is fear. Our fears can become lord over us.

Many Christians allow fear to hold them back from life's greatest mission. If you are a Christian, you have the life preserver that people need. The bible says we have been given the ministry of reconciliation (2 Corinthians 5:18). We have a task, a commission, and a commandment to share our faith with others. We do this from a platform of love and not self-righteousness.

It will only take a few moments in the after-life to have all our priorities and values polarized. Many things we value and give high regard to in this life will suddenly become worthless in eternity. We will not wish that we had worked harder on earth to gain more wealth.

Jesus came to seek and save that which is lost (Luke 19:10). He did not come looking for gold or silver, he came seeking the true treasure: the souls of men. Jesus gave us light so it can shine and told us not to hide it (Matthew 5:14-16). The world will make you feel ashamed because of your Christian beliefs and values. This causes some to shrink back from being a witness. When we do this, whom are we serving? Jesus warned his disciples of this temptation.

And do not fear those who kill the body but cannot kill the soul. Rather fear him who can destroy both soul and body in hell. Matthew 10:28 ESV

For whoever is ashamed of me and of my words in this adulterous and sinful generation, of him will the Son of Man also be ashamed when he comes in the glory of his Father with the holy angels. Mark 8:38 ESV

For am I now seeking the approval of man, or of God? Or am I trying to please man? If I were still trying to please man, I would not be a servant of Christ. Galatians 1:10 ESV

Fear of facing the truth

There is an old saying that "Ignorance is bliss." We create a false sense of security by avoiding painful reality. Fear is not the only factor here, but it is part of the mix. We do not want to face some truths in life because of what it might mean. This includes being afraid of admitting fear is an issue in our lives. We fear facing the truth about ourselves. Many people live a superficial outward existence and never peer on the inside of their own heart. The power of God's word can peal back the covers and force us to face who we really are. This is why going to church makes some people uncomfortable.

Fear will cause us to ignore or avoid confronting problems in life. Maybe it is our teenager who we sense is going down the wrong path. We refuse to confront the situation because of the fear of finding out what they are really doing. Some parents fear their kids. They do not want to say "no" to their children or discipline them in any way for fear of pushing them away. Maybe it is a marriage partner that is becoming distant. We are afraid of what we might find, afraid of the reaction or the fallout, afraid to face our own failure. So, we act like everything is fine and never reach out to draw them close again.

It might be much easier to remain silent, but it is not the loving thing to do. The bible says we are to "speak the truth in love (Ephesians 4:15)."

Giving an honest answer is a sign of true friendship. Proverbs 24:26 CEV

This is not a license to speak whatever comes to mind. Truth and opinion are not the same things. Neither is lack of conflict the same thing as harmony. If we gloss over every issue that might cause tension or discomfort, relationships will remain shallow at best.

Fear is often the force behind self-preservation. The survival instinct focuses inward. We are worried about what might happen to us or what people will think of us. However, if we truly love the people in our lives, we cannot let fear keep us from doing the necessary. Whether or not we are comfortable with confrontation is not the issue. There is a time to cast aside fear for personal safety and reach out to those who need rescuing. The effort might not be successful. Yes, we might end up looking like the bad guy. We might get burned in the process. Nevertheless, fear is not an excuse for avoiding responsibility. If we ignore the problems and pretend they do not exist, we only allow them to grow deeper and more complex. The earlier we deal with issues, the easier it is to affect change.

The prison of fear

Rick Warren, in his book The Purpose Driven Life, said this about fear: "Regardless of the cause, fear-driven people often miss great opportunities because they're afraid to venture out. Instead they play it safe, avoiding risks and trying to maintain the status quo. Fear is a self-imposed prison that will keep you from becoming what God intends for you to be." **2.**

There are many things that people allow to hold them in a self-imposed prison. These include the fear of

Failure

Rejection

Change

Success

Getting hurt

Going without

Giving 100 percent

Abandonment

Commitment

Getting ripped off

Confrontation

Not measuring up

Getting old

Sickness

Ridicule

We were not born with courage, but neither are we born with fear. Fear is a learned behavior. It begins when the adults in our lives are constantly saying, "Be careful!"

Lisa Jimenez, in her book Conquer Fear, tells it this way: Picture this: A one-year-old boy sees a set of stairs for the first time. What do you think went through his mind as he stood looking up at this exciting, new thing? (If you have ever been around kids, you know!) He probably thought to himself, "Wow! I've got to get to the top!"

He didn't stand at the bottom and think, "I'd like to get to the top, but I'd better not. I might get hurt." Or, "What would my mom say? I might get in trouble." He didn't stand at the bottom and think, "I want to get to the top!...but what would my friends say about me? They might laugh at me." He didn't tell himself any of these negatives. No! He just began. He focused on his goal and did not allow any negative thought to break his concentration on this wonderful new apparatus. **3.**

You and I were once that child uninhibited by fear and

intimidation. Toddlers can be deposited into a room with other children they have never met and within minutes be playing with each other like they grew up together. There is no fear of what others think or desire to look cool and fit in. Kids do not examine all the angles and "what ifs" in a situation. They just boldly blaze forward into life's adventure.

What happened to us? Where did that risk-taking part of our character go? Life happens! Failure, rejection, circumstance, culture, etc., all work to teach us to be more careful. We call it wisdom, but all too often it is just the fear of getting hurt or making mistakes. Obviously, we do learn some things along the way. But instead of using that knowledge and applying it to risk-taking, we labor to avoid challenges all together. Our fears hold us back from growing into what God intended us to be. We put dreams and desire for accomplishment on the shelf and opt for a safer existence.

Ann Landers, the newspaper columnist, was once asked, "Out of all the thousands of letters you receive each month, what problem is most dominant in people's lives?" Her answer was immediate. "It's fear! The one thing that keeps people from the life they dream of is fear. People live every day in their fear. They're afraid of losing their wealth. They're afraid of losing their loved ones. They're afraid of being themselves. They're afraid of growing up and being responsible. They're afraid of making the wrong decision. They're afraid of making a commitment. They're afraid of life itself!" **4.** Wow!

I have a friend who is the pastor of a good-sized church in a large city full of opportunity. Before becoming the pastor, he owned a company that did property appraisals. He had employed several people from the church as appraisers and the business was doing quite well. When he became senior pastor, he felt the need to give himself full-time to the ministry. So, out of good will, he offered to *give* the business to these church members. No doubt, these saints had been praying for blessing and provision. Here was the miracle open door. This pastor was going to hand over all the accounts and let them have the company. But they said no! It is one thing to appraise property and another thing all together to deal with corporate executives from investment firms and insurance companies to maintain accounts and expand the business.

Fear held them back. They were afraid to step out and do something beyond their comfort zones. What were they afraid of exactly? Were one of these business owners going to do them physical harm? Of course not! What is the absolute worst thing that could happen? Rejection? Failure? Would not the reward outweigh the risk? How many times have you not taken advantage of an opportunity because of fear? It is scary to think about.

We don't always identify fear as the issue holding us back because our palms are not sweating and our knees are not knocking. But fear can be a simple subtle voice in our head that points out our weaknesses and inability. All of us have dreams and goals we would like to accomplish, but we are held back from even trying many times because we listen to those voices. "Who do you think you are really? You could never do that! You could never be that!" Peter T. McIntyre said, "Confidence comes not from always being right, but from not fearing to be wrong." **5.**

Think of all the books never written, businesses never started, and relationships that never developed because people were held back by fear and insecurity. What about the souls never touched by the gospel because somebody was too intimidated to share their faith? Are there nations that have never been reached because of an unwillingness on the part of a would-be missionary to take the risk?

Remember the children of Israel on the banks of the Jordan River? The other side of that river is the land promised to them by God himself; a land of fruitfulness and abundance, provision and pleasure. All they have to do is drive out the inhabitants. God promised he would help them, but the voices of doubt prevailed. "There are giants in the land. We are like grasshoppers in their sight and in our sight also." Fear has the ability to substantially warp the perception of reality. Reality was that the citizens of the land were rightfully fearful of Israel. They knew of how God had performed miracles to bring Israel out of Egypt. Nevertheless, Israel listened to the "evil report" and fear swept through the camp. They made the decision to not enter the promised land based on their fears (Numbers 13).

Fear has been described as **F**alse **E**vidence **A**ppearing **R**eal. **6.** We cannot think clearly or rationally when fear grips us. Edmund Burke said, "No passion so effectually robs the mind of all its powers of acting and reasoning as fear." **7.** Fear is a rash like the measles or chicken pox. You do not get just one spot, it comes in bunches. Fear spreads through our personality and infects our attitude, robs us of hope, hinders our decision-making and affects our relationships. Most people do not stand and confront the issues they fear; they spend their entire life running instead.

I love the analogy of the eagle with her little eaglets. These eaglets are born into a nest full of soft cozy surroundings. The mother delivers food to their penthouse nest high up on the side of the cliff. The eaglets live a life of eating and sleeping. But mom knows they will never fly if they do not leave the nest, and they will never leave the nest until it becomes uncomfortable. So, mom begins to remove the soft cozy elements of the their surroundings. Now when the eaglets roll over sticks and sharp objects prick them. Eventually mom literally pushes the eaglet out of the nest into a free fall. She will catch the young bird before it hits the ground, but the instinct of fear teaches this baby to fly pretty quickly. We will never spread our wings and fly if we are unwilling to leave the familiar.

Fear can hold us back from what we are created to do. Everyone can look at the eagle and know it was created to fly. They function by instinct. You have never heard of an eagle that does not fly because of fear. An eagle will reach its full potential. It will fly as high as it possibly can. God created you and I to do amazing things as well. However, we must be determined not to let fear keep us from soaring to the heights of what God created us to be.

Johannesburg

I was a missionary in South Africa from 1998-2003. Fear was a daily battle I faced. In my opinion, the prevailing atmosphere in that nation is fear. We lived in Johannesburg, where the crime rate is one of the highest in the world. People there live in fortresses. Walls, often with electric fences on top, surround homes. Windows have rod iron cages or bars and most yards have at least one man-eating dog. Home surveillance and security is a huge business. A company that promised response in 3 minutes or less monitored the alarm on our house. They accomplished this by having armed guards parked throughout the area, waiting for a call. Our house also had a cage door on the hallway going back to the bedrooms that we could lock at night. All this gave new meaning to "the prison of fear."

Carjacking is one issue I had never even heard of before living there. Most often it happens at a traffic light. The unsuspecting motorist is shot through the windshield or side window and dragged from the car to be stolen. Especially people driving alone, women, and ignorant tourist are targeted. In order to combat this, people run red lights at night when they cannot see who is lurking in the shadows. The police actually encourage this. Every commute was tainted with fear.

Stories of murder and mayhem were endless and unnerving. My landlord rented his house to us because he had taken a job on the opposite side of town. He told me of the great deal he had gotten on a home purchase in that new area. The discounted house had been empty, so a guard had been hired to stay there until it was sold. Somebody broke into the house, beat up the guard and then hung him by the neck in the living room. This senseless crime brought the price of the home down.

Our mission was in a township called SOWETO. The word is an acronym for South West Township. Famous South Africans such as Nelson Mandela and Bishop Tutu were from this area. During the years of Apartheid, it was the scene of a lot of violence and bloodshed. Especially in the run-up to democracy, SOWETO was very unstable and dangerous. Under the former laws of separation, whites like me were not allowed to go in these township areas. Even though these laws have changed, people's hearts remain the same. I found that fear and ignorance are the motivating factors behind the prejudice.

In the "European" area, my accent gave away that I was a foreigner. Of course, everybody wants to tell the foreigner about all the crime and violence and warn him to be careful. Somewhere in the conversation, they would inquire why I was in the country. I loved to say I had a mission in SOWETO. Just seeing the look of terror that would sweep over people's faces became a perverse pleasure. After an awkward moment they would recover and say something like, "Oh, that is nice," and then run off to tell somebody about the dumb American that will soon be dead. I am not saying you should never heed a warning or that you should not be careful. We incorporated a lot of caution into our routines in South Africa. However, I knew God had called me to be there and could not let the voices of fear keep me from the task.

What is fear doing to YOU?

To what voices are you listening? I think about the years I spent as a missionary in SOWETO and know it was one of the highlights of my entire life. The fruitfulness and personal fulfillment were incredible. The people there are some of the most loving and wonderful people on the planet. I would have missed this had I listened to the voices of fear. Many allow fear to hold them back from taking any step of faith, from obedience, and from the fruitfulness they know God has called them to. They will not share their faith for fear of what people might say of them. They will not give to a level of sacrifice for fear of going without. They will not ask God for specific things like healing the sick for fear it will not happen. They will not dare to risk for fear of failure.

The list goes on and on. It is like a crow sitting up on a power line, staring out at an endless cornfield with enough food to feed on for the rest of his life. No more scrounging, no more struggling, and no more fighting other crows over a scrap from a trashcan. It is all here. But, the crow sits on the power line not making a move. Why? In the middle of the field is a scarecrow. Now, we know this is only a couple of broom sticks tied together like a cross, the farmers old clothes stuffed with old under garments and an old hat on top. However, in the mind of the crow it is an enemy, a threat to his life, an obstacle that cannot be overcome. And so the crow sits there salivating, dreaming, wishing…but not moving because of fear.

Life consists of choices. The choices we make are seeds that bear fruit in our future. Some choices are crossroads that determine destiny; defining moments that galvanize who we are and characterize our life. Abraham was asked to sacrifice his son Isaac (Genesis 22). God was testing Abraham's faith and commitment. Can you imagine having to make this kind of choice? Abraham takes his son to Mount Moriah, prepares an altar of sacrifice and lays young Isaac on top. He is about to kill the son of promise in obedience when God stops him. "Do not lay your hand on the lad, or do anything to him; for now I know that you fear God, since you have not withheld your son, your only son, from Me." This became a defining moment in Abraham's life. He is known as the "father of faith" because of this event. At this point God reconfirmed his covenant to make Abraham the father of a great nation.

Think about defining moments in your own life. Has timidity become the reaction that characterizes who you are? Are you held back from obedience to God by fear, doubt and unbelief? Is this who you want to be? There is hope for change! If choices took you down this road, then you can make a choice that will change your direction.

For this reason I remind you to fan into flame the gift of God, which is in you through the laying on of my hands. For God did not give us a spirit of timidity, but a spirit of power, of love and of self-discipline. 2 Timothy 1:6-7 NIV

Timothy was a missionary. I can tell you from experience that when living in a foreign country everything is magnified: different culture, different language, customs, money, etc. In some places, as in South Africa, they drive on the wrong side of the road from the wrong side of the car. It is intimidating! Timothy was laboring as a missionary in Ephesus. This is the city where a riot took place and the apostle Paul was snuck out of town so he would not be killed (Acts 19). Now Paul is writing to Timothy from prison, where he has been thrown for preaching the gospel, "God has not given us the spirit of fear." Timothy was there, but he was not fulfilling his purpose. He was silent perhaps. Maybe he was afraid to confront the false doctrines that were being spread. It is possible he was intimidated by the religious leaders of the city. Timothy was bold when Paul was around, but now he is by himself. Who knows all the reasoning and excuses swirling around in Timothy's head? Paul identifies it as a spirit of fear or timidity that was paralyzing Timothy.

What has you intimidated? What in your mind has been blown out of proportion and has you fearful? What is it that is holding you back? The first step in overcoming is identifying it and calling it what it is. We need to take our feelings of fear to the Lord and ask Him to help us identify why we are fearful. We must then commit those fears to Him. We must determine that fear is not going to define who we are and what we do in life.

This is where courage begins.

PART 2 - COURAGE

Be of good courage, and he shall strengthen your heart, all you who hope in the LORD. Psalms 31:24 NKJV

Courage is a choice. Many wrongly think they have no courage because they feel fear. As we have said, fear is a natural God given emotion. Courage is not the absence of fear, it is the choice to proceed in spite of the fear you feel.

We have all known people who seem fearless. They boldly go into situations that make others quiver. However, fearlessness is not reality. Rambo-types are only in the movies. David valiantly goes against the nine-foot Goliath with a sling and 5 smooth stones (1 Samuel 17). While the army of Israel is allowing fear to rule the moment, David says, "Who is this uncircumcised Philistine that would defy the living God." It is inspiring! Did David feel fear? Of course he did. However, he put his fears aside and did what needed to be done. That is courage.

Consider other heroes of history. Susan B. Anthony was the first woman to vote in America. It was not legal for her to do so, but it was right. In 1872 she boldly walked into a voting booth and cast her vote, while men stood all around with gaping mouths. Was she scared? Of course, but she was determined. In 1955, Rosa Parks refused to move to the back of the bus because of her skin color. Was she scared? Of course, she was scared. She chose courage over fear. It did not matter to her what everybody else was doing at the time. Despite what was considered proper or legal, she was determined.

General George Patton was praised for his bravery by a governor in Sicily. The general replied, "Sir, I am not a brave man...the truth is I am an utter craven coward. I have never been within the sound of gunshot or in sight of battle in my whole life that I was not so scared that I had sweat in the palms of my hands." Wait a minute. How could he do what he did if he was filled with fear? He writes in his autobiography, "I learned very early in my life never to take counsel of my fears." **1.** That is courage! Courage is not the absence of fear; it is the refusal to be ruled by your fears.

Meek VS Timid

Jesus said that the meek shall inherit the earth (Matthew 5:5). Many interpret this word "meek" as weak or timid. Being bold, in their definition, is not a Christian virtue. They think we are to be doormats, pushed around, taken advantage of, stepped over, and used. To them, asserting yourself would be selfish. Somehow, in their view, God will allow us to inherit the earth if we take this posture.

I do not believe that meek means timid or weak. Moses was called the meekest man on the earth (Numbers 12:3). This same Moses went into the throne room of the most powerful leader in the world at the time and demanded he let the children of Israel go. The word timid does not adequately describe that action. This is not a weak, quiet little request; Moses demands with authority and pronounces curses and judgment. And, it does not end there. I know God is the miracle power behind all that happens in this story, but you have to give Moses credit for having a lot of guts. Moses leads the people out of Egypt, parts the Red Sea, heals the bitter water, brings water out of a rock, defeats the Amalekites in battle, confronts idolatry and rebellion in the ranks, goes forty days without food, and stands in the presence of God to receive the ten commandments. Moses was not a weak and timid man. He was a strong and bold leader who God anointed to do His work.

David was a man of war; a bold and courageous soldier. Prior to the victory over Goliath, he had killed a lion and a bear when they tried to attack his sheep. The bridal price he paid for Michal, Saul's daughter, was two hundred Philistine foreskins (1 Samuel 18:27). He was not a timid man. Yet, David speaks of being meek in the book of Psalms.

The meek will He guide in judgment: and the meek will He teach His way. Psalms 25:9 KJV

David was labeled in the bible as a man after God's own heart. He writes most of the praise Psalms that we sing in church today. This would seem to some people to be a personality conflict. Simply, David was a brave man with a tender heart toward God.

Jesus was meek, yet timid is not a word you can use to describe his life. Jesus was a carpenter by trade. Even today, with all the power tools we have available, this is hard work. He probably looked more like a construction worker than the soft portraits that artist have given us through the centuries. Jesus on several occasions confronted the religious leaders of the day, publicly denouncing their hypocrisy. He made a whip and drove the moneychangers out of the temple (Matthew 21). I can picture Him turning over tables, opening the birdcages, driving the livestock, and wreaking havoc. We would probably call this vandalism. He cried out, "My Father's house is to be a house of prayer and you have made it a den of thieves." Jesus was not exactly politically correct and he offended people on several occasions. So much for being weak and timid!

Paul the apostle was meek. If meekness is a Christian virtue, then the man who wrote most of the New Testament surely was meek. Yet, timid is not a word you can use to describe his life as an evangelist. He started more than one riot in his career by denouncing idolatry and religious hypocrisy. It was not his weak, timid approach that got him thrown in jail, stoned, beaten, and chased out of town. This is also the guy that said we are to follow his example (1 Corinthians 11:1).

You see, timidity is not a virtue. Timidity is just a fancy word for fear and insecurity. You can call it shy, quiet, bashful, or make excuses for it and say, "It is just the way I am." But, the reality is, our approach to life is a choice we make. We do not have to be fearful and insecure.

Life takes courage. Courage is the choice to proceed through your anxiety. Timidity will keep you from everything valuable that life has to offer. There are very talented people who never reach their full potential because of fear. The prize does not always go to the most qualified, but often to the most bold. This is true in every area of life. The young upstart salesperson lands the big account because he did not listen to the veterans who said it could not be done. The person willing to take the risk and start a business, regardless of the necessary sacrifice, ends up the success. Musicians, artists, authors, and athletes, all have to swallow their fears, turn off the negative voices, and go for it. It may not elevate them to hero status, but it is an act of courage.

What is it that you want to accomplish in life? What dream have you put on hold because of timidity? You must identify fear as what is holding you back and call it what it is. This sounds so simple, but many never admit it. They blame, rationalize and make excuse why they do not take the plunge forward. They point at every factor and circumstance in life to explain their mediocrity. Pride will not allow them to call it fear. It takes courage to step outside your comfort zone!

SOWETO

One night, there were about thirty of us who were putting away equipment at the church after we had showed an evangelistic movie in a neighborhood park. I had only been in South Africa a few months at the time. I noticed that work ceased, everyone was quiet and staring at me with fear in their eyes. One young man finally spoke up and I was told there were some men outside that wanted to talk to me. I started to go out when they stopped me and said, "No pastor, these are bad men." I said, "Okay, we will all go out and talk to them."

I stepped outside the tent with the whole group behind me. Four men had driven up in two cars and they asked to talk to me in private. Yeah right! I said, "These are all church members and whatever you have to say they can hear also." These men announced that they did not like the church and were giving me twenty-four hours to pack up and leave.

Sometimes, when you are a leader, you have to act brave even when you feel fearful. People are watching to see what you are going to do and will follow your lead.

I said, "We have a right to be here. Jesus called us to go into all the world and preach the gospel. This is a mandate from a higher authority than you and we are not leaving." They threatened some more, got in their cars and left. As soon as they drove off, several girls in our group started crying. It turns out these men were some well-known political thugs and one was identified as a hit man. I said, "Listen, the devil is a liar! The church is here to stay. We are not going anywhere. God is going to help us."

We prayed against a spirit of fear. I then casually gathered my family and drove off (at record speed). For the next three weeks I drove home a different way from church every night. I never found out exactly what the deal was behind the threat. One of the women in the church had some political influence and the thugs were called off. I concluded it was just a demonically inspired effort to intimidate us from being there.

On another occasion, during our first few months in South Africa, we set up our sound equipment in a busy shopping area and had some people from the church do rap songs with evangelistic lyrics. They were actually very talented. In between songs, church members gave testimony to what God had done in their lives. Even though English is understood by most, these were always very powerful times because they could share the gospel in the native languages of Zulu, Setswana, and Nkoza. I took the microphone and preached for a minute or two in English. I mentioned that Jesus is risen from the dead, while other religious figures were still in the grave.

From nowhere, a Muslim man came forward and started poking his finger in my chest, demanding that I apologize to the prophet. Not only did my skin color make me stand out like a neon light, on this day, I was wearing a t-shirt that said "Alaska" across the front. It was obvious to him I was from "evil" America. He was screaming at me that he would die for the prophet. I interpreted that to mean he would kill for the prophet. Others from the shopping center started gathering and yelling back at him to let us preach. Of course, all the church members have now come in close behind me as well. Into this brewing riot, a van pulls up right in front of our stage area. The sliding door opened and this man steps out with his hand in his pocket. When I remember this event, it is always in slow motion. In my mind, I could picture this person pulling out an automatic weapon and spraying all of us down dead. There was nowhere to hide. The guy came right for me, pulled his hand out of his pocket, stuck his finger in my chest and said, "You have offended the prophet." Somehow I backed out of the crowd, slipped into a car and was driven out of there. It is hard to describe the fear that you are now a target, but that is exactly how I felt. It took a while before I went back into this particular area, but we continued to do street meetings weekly.

One day, I was driving through the township area in my 1976 VW Beetle when I heard a loud pop. This is not a good place to have a flat tire. In the area of the church, I was well known, but here, I am just a Mulungu (word for "white man" in Zulu) out of place. I pulled over, got out and circled the car to access the damage. All the tires looked good. I thought maybe a rock hit one of the headlights so I went to the front of the car but found them to be okay. By now, people are staring. As I was about to get back in the car, I noticed a hole in the side of the car. I was upset because I just had this car painted. I looked closer and realized it was a bullet hole. Somebody shot my car right on the driver side behind the front fender. I started looking around to determine the angle it came from. I can be a little slow catching on sometimes, but eventually it sinks in that perhaps if somebody shot at my car I should get out of there. I am sure I set a speed record for VW Beetles.

Our church meeting place was a big tent. At one end, we had an outside portable latrine for members to use. One night a couple of girls were robbed at gunpoint while standing in line to use it. From then on, we had ushers escort people to use the outhouse. On another occasion, a couple got robbed at gunpoint right in front of the tent. The robbers approached the couple from out of the darkness, demanded the girl, the book (which happened to be the bible) and his wallet. Our member shoved the girl forward and told her to run to the church about 50 yards away. The robbers then shot him in the foot, took his bible and ran off.

We were in a community that had a long history of violence and upheaval. There were many stories told by the older people in our church of dead bodies in the streets, racial oppression, political infighting, and rioting.

A day that stands out in South African history is June 16, 1976. The government had passed a law that half of all classes in secondary schools must be taught in Afrikaans. The students and teachers in the township considered this the "language of the oppressors." Pleadings and petitions by parents and teachers had fallen on deaf ears. Middle school children in SOWETO decided to protest with a peaceful rally. The plan was to march from the different schools to a central gathering place. They held signs that read in English, "to hell with Afrikaans," and other such sayings. The police, wearing riot gear and armed for battle, confronted the students and warned them to disperse. This sparked song, dance and chanting from the children as they kept on marching. The police opened fire on the eleven, twelve and thirteen year old students, killing estimates as high as six hundred. One young boy who was killed, named Hector Pieterson, was caught on film as he was being carried in the arms of a young man, his sister running at their side, crying hysterically. This photo went around the world and sparked international pressure against the Apartheid government. There is a memorial now in SOWETO honoring Hector as a martyr for the struggle. At the time, this event sparked days of rioting and bloodshed, which spread to the other townships of South Africa. The very ground that our tent was set up on had been a war zone. The government buildings that had stood there were attacked and burned to the ground by angry protestors.

The stories go on and on. I had to decide that I was not going to live by fear. This is the place God was calling me. I had to make a choice. I had to recognize the strategy of the enemy to intimidate me and keep me from God's calling.

Fear has a voice!

I have come to a conclusion and I think is true in most circumstances we fear: Our imagination exaggerates. So many people told us we would be killed if we went into SOWETO. The stories were unending. My mind developed a picture of what it was going to be like, but once we stepped into the ministry there, I discovered that it was nothing like people had said. From then on, when people predicted doom, I started asking them if they had ever been into the township. Very, very few had. It was actually illegal for European decent citizens to enter into SOWETO during the Apartheid era. People believed the propaganda of government newspaper and TV media (This is a great case study for the value of the freedom of press). The fuel of prejudice is fear and ignorance.

What we found in Zone 2 Meadowlands, SOWETO were people just like every other person on the planet. They have feelings, wants, passions, and goals. Ironically, people from our church felt safe in their neighborhood and feared going into central Johannesburg. The stories they told of the dangers in downtown were similar to what was being said about their area.

When we listen to these reports and our imagination takes over. We then call it wise to stay in our place and not venture out. Your place might be poverty, a dead end job, mediocrity, boredom, or loneliness. It is the place where you feel safe because you are familiar with it. Security is a real need in life. However, it often is the very thing holding us back from achievement. The comfort zone is so...comfortable.

Sometimes those voices we hear are our own. Survival is a basic element of human nature. The limbic brain refers to the system in our mind that is the seat of instinct, subconscious habits, and attitudes. This is referred to sometimes as the "animal brain." It is that part of the brain where the voices of fear and doubt come from. "You can't do this. You are going to fail. Who do you think you are? Run for your life." This is the voice of self-preservation.

Have you ever stopped and listened to yourself? What are you saying? Do your words inspire courage and faith in those around you? Perhaps your words are the very reason you are fearful of going forward. Is all your doubt coming out of your mouth? Words are spiritual. Jesus said, "My words are spirit and they are life (John 6:63)." Just as God created the world by his word, we create an atmosphere in our lives by the words we speak. I know this has been taken to the extreme in some circles, but there is truth here nonetheless. Have you ever walked into a room where somebody was arguing and you can feel it immediately? The conversation has stopped but the atmosphere remains. In the same way, we are creating an atmosphere of faith or doubt in our homes with the words we speak. Do our words build up faith and confidence in God? Do we inspire hope for the future and comfort in His promise? Jesus said that words come from the heart and reveal what is on the inside (Matthew 15:18). If fear is resident in your heart, it will come out of your mouth. Our confession seals the deal, so to speak, and establishes something in our life. Rather than giving voice to fear, we should confess the promises of God!

For we all stumble in many ways. And if anyone does not stumble in what he says, he is a perfect man, able also to bridle his whole body. If we put bits into the mouths of horses so that they obey us, we guide their whole bodies as well. Look at the ships also: though they are so large and are driven by strong winds, they are guided by a very small rudder wherever the will of the pilot directs. So also the tongue is a small member, yet it boasts of great things. How great a forest is set ablaze by such a small fire! And the tongue is a fire, a world of unrighteousness. The tongue is set among our members, staining the whole body, setting on fire the entire course of life, and set on fire by hell. For every kind of beast and bird, of reptile and sea creature, can be tamed and has been tamed by mankind, but no human being can tame the tongue. It is a restless evil, full of deadly poison. With it we bless our Lord and Father, and with it we curse people who are made in the likeness of God. From the same mouth come blessing and cursing. My brothers, these things ought not to be so. Does a spring pour forth from the same opening both fresh and salt water? Can a fig tree, my brothers, bear olives, or a grapevine produce figs? Neither can a salt pond yield fresh water. James 3:2-12 ESV

James makes some powerful observations about the tongue and the words that come out of our mouths. Just like a bit in a horse's mouth is used to steer, our words have the power to determine direction. Words are like seeds that we are planting. You will reap what you sow! What direction are your words taking you? Do you talk about doing God's will and accomplishing what He has for you? Or, do you talk about your plans and your priorities? Do your words point you and your family in the direction of eternal things?

James says that the rudder on a ship is small and yet guides this ship through the stormy waters. What do you talk about during the storms of life? Do you confess God's promises? Do your words inspire courage and faith to believe God? Or, do you talk about the obstacles and the enemies?

Maybe you send out a mixed message. James talks about bitter and sweet water coming out of a spring at the same time. You speak faith one day and discouragement the next. The mixed message is creating confusion. Your wife would love to follow you, but she is not sure where you are going! You must nurture courage in those you are leading. The bible says that faith comes by hearing the Word (Romans 10:17). We need to speak His promises. You will reap a harvest from the words you are planting.

Death and life are in the power of the tongue, and those who love it will eat its fruit. Proverbs 18:21 NKJV

Jericho was a walled city in the land promised to the children of Israel. It was the first city they faced in an attempt to conquer. God gives an unusual battle plan to Joshua. They are to walk around the city once each day for six days. On the seventh day, they are to walk around the city seven times and then shout. God told Joshua, when they shouted the walls would come down flat and they could then take the city.

31

Joshua has to relay this plan to the people and inspire courage to accomplish the task. When Joshua tells the people the plan, he adds something to it. He commands silence for the seven days they are to walk around the city (Joshua 6:10). It is interesting that this came from Joshua and not from God.

Why this command for silence? Joshua was with the children of Israel forty years earlier when they heard the evil report of unbelief given by ten of the twelve men that had spied out the promise land and caused the people of God to give into the spirit of fear (Numbers 13). Joshua and Caleb were the two who confessed faith and confidence in God.

Joshua knew very well that given the chance, the people could talk themselves out of doing the will of God. Imagine walking around the city on day one. There would be a few complainers and a little bit of grumbling. Day two would be worse, but by day three it would be full on rebellion and debate. When it was time to walk around the city on day four, half the people would stay in their tents. Joshua could see this in advance and so he commanded them to say nothing.

Sometimes the best approach to a situation is to shut your mouth. We have the capability of talking ourselves out of doing what is right. We make excuse and justify our position until it sounds good to us. We must learn not to give voice to our fears.

David and Goliath

Goliath intimidated the army of Israel into inaction by taunting them with threatening words. David comes on the scene and is appalled that the giant is having this affect on these men of valor.

And all the men of Israel, when they saw the man, fled from him and were dreadfully afraid. 1 Samuel 17:24 NKJV

David says, "I will fight the giant." Immediately, people are there to talk him out of it. "You are too young. You are not a warrior. You have no armor." Even King Saul said, "You can't do this." But, look at the words that David speaks.

But David said to Saul, "Your servant used to keep sheep for his father. And when there came a lion, or a bear, and took a lamb from the flock, I went after him and struck him and delivered it out of his mouth. And if he arose against me, I caught him by his beard and struck him and killed him. Your servant has struck down both lions and bears, and this uncircumcised Philistine shall be like one of them, for he has defied the armies of the living God." And David said, "The LORD who delivered me from the paw of the lion and from the paw of the bear will deliver me from the hand of this Philistine." ...Then David said to the Philistine, "You come to me with a sword and with a spear and with a javelin, but I come to you in the name of the LORD of hosts, the God of the armies of Israel, whom you have defied. This day the LORD will deliver you into my hand, and I will strike you down and cut off your head. And I will give the dead bodies of the host of the Philistines this day to the birds of the air and to the wild beasts of the earth, that all the earth may know that there is a God in Israel, and that all this assembly may know that the LORD saves not with sword and spear. For the battle is the LORD's, and he will give you into our hand." 1 Samuel 17:34-47 ESV

David faces his fear with courage. We call this bravery. This is not just having a positive mental attitude or confession. This is not trash talk before a boxing match or sporting event.

David has a source of strength beyond himself. He has a reason to feel brave and confident. He says, "The battle belongs to the Lord." He trusts in God to help him win the victory. If you are trusting in your own strength to face the giants in your life then you should be afraid of defeat. To trust the Lord means putting the fight in His hand and believing for a supernatural miracle result.

...but the people that do know their God shall be strong, and do exploits.
Daniel 11:32 KJV

Whine and cheese

Life comes with conflict and difficulty. Warfare is such a great analogy of life and Christianity. Sometimes we must wage war to gain possession of territory and advance the kingdom. Other times we must fight to maintain ground already conquered. I am not suggesting we wage war for no reason. Of course, peaceful solutions are wonderful and we should pursue them. But generally speaking, the passive of our world serve the aggressive. Sometimes we must engage in battle. Courage is a necessary element.

Many spend all their energy feeling sorry for themselves. This is one of the most destructive forces in the human personality. Whining about your circumstances will not change them. Listing all the reasons you have it bad and cannot possibly win will not give you victory in the battles of life. Self-pity is fertile ground for demonically inspired selfishness. Remember when Jesus told his disciples that he would be killed in Jerusalem but raised on the third day? Peter pulled Jesus aside and rebuked him. "Pity yourself" is the phrase one translation uses. Jesus says, "Get behind me Satan (Matthew 16:23)." Wow! Was Jesus in a bad mood or what? The whisper of self-pity is the devil's voice. In this frame of mind, people give in to discouragement and even depression. Instead of boldly going forward, they curl up in defeat. Self-pity, blame and the victim mentality will rob you of courage.

Tom Brokaw, in his book The Greatest Generation, tells of war veteran Tom Broderick: in WWII, he was shot through the head by a German sniper and left blind. After the initial shock and confusion, he set out to put his life back together. He learned Braille, learned how to type and started an insurance business. He refused even to put a handicap sticker on his car because he did not want to use that label as a crutch. "What's a handicap? I don't have a handicap." He is not bitter like many today that blame everybody else. "It was my own fault for getting up too high in the foxhole. That happens sometimes." **2.**

Jehoshaphat was afraid of the enemy armies that were coming to attack him and he prayed for courage (2 Chronicles 20). He did not pray all the problems in life would go away. He did not whine, "It's not fair." No, life is not fair. Jehoshaphat points out that the approaching enemies are returning evil for good.

And now behold, the men of Ammon and Moab and Mount Seir, whom you would not let Israel invade when they came from the land of Egypt, and whom they avoided and did not destroy. Behold, they reward us by coming to drive us out of your possession, which you have given us to inherit. 2 Chronicles 20:10-11 ESV

This is life. The strong oppress the weak. Corruption prevails over righteousness. Deception pushes out truth. It is not fair. However, there is a righteous God in heaven who will involve himself in the affairs of this world on the behalf of his people. Jehoshaphat understood this. He prayed for courage and strength and God responds to this prayer.

And he said, "Listen, all Judah and inhabitants of Jerusalem and King Jehoshaphat: Thus says the LORD to you, 'Do not be afraid and do not be dismayed at this great horde, for the battle is not yours but God's. ...You will not need to fight in this battle. Stand firm, hold your position, and see the salvation of the LORD on your behalf, O Judah and Jerusalem.' Do not be afraid and do not be dismayed. Tomorrow go out against them, and the LORD will be with you." 2 Chronicles 20:15-17 ESV

I think we should take note of the battle strategy that Jehoshaphat uses. He lines up the choir on the front line and they lead the army into battle singing and worshiping. As soon as they began to sing praise, God sent confusion into the enemy's camp so that they turned on each other. Now, I have heard choirs that confused me as well, but this is not about bad singing, this is a miracle. When the army of Israel got to the battlefield there was nothing but dead bodies (2 Chronicles 20:22-24). God gave them the victory as promised. When we worship rather than whine, God is magnified in our circumstances instead of fear and self-pity.

Fear Not!

Fear and courage are opposites. The Bible repeatedly encourages us not to be fearful. It says three hundred fifty-five times, "Fear not." God speaks to Joshua, "Be strong and of good courage;

do not be afraid, nor be dismayed, for the Lord your God is with you wherever you go (Joshua 1:9)." God knows we are tempted to be fearful.

Jesus was tempted with fear in the garden of Gethsemane. He prayed, "Father, if it is your will, take this cup from me; nevertheless, not my will but yours be done (Matthew 26:39)." The angel came and strengthened Him. He did not give into fear, but faced the cross with the courage and strength that God supplied.

The Bible promises us that we will never be tempted beyond our ability to handle it and with every temptation, there is a way of escape (1 Corinthians 10:13). That includes the temptation to let fear rule your life and circumstance. You do not have to react in fear. You can let God strengthen you and give you courage.

We think fear is a valid excuse for not doing what we should. "I was afraid!" This is the same mentality as one who stands before a judge in court and blames anger for his violent crime. Emotion is not an excuse for disobedience! Israel would not cross the Jordan River and go into the promise land because of fear. God called it rebellion. The New Testament refers to this day as the day of provocation (Hebrews 3:8). It may seem unsympathetic to you, but the reason is simply that God will supply all your need according to His riches in glory, including courage. Fear is not an excuse!

Courage is the choice to proceed in spite of our fears. It is not a feeling that overcomes us. The command to have courage is similar to other commands in the bible that require obedience regardless of emotion. Forgiveness, for example, is not a feeling; it is what God tells us we must do. If you take the step to forgive, the feelings will come later. Love is not a feeling. Obviously, there are emotions connected with love, but love is commitment. When you are faithful to put aside selfishness and love people, then the feelings come.

Courage is the same. When you obey God in going forward with his call and plan for your life, then the strength will come. Ten Lepers came to Jesus for healing and he told them to go show themselves to the priests. On the way, they received healing (Luke 17:12). Jesus told the crippled man by the pool of Bethesda to get up. As he obeyed, he was healed (John 5:8). Obedience brought the miracle.

Maybe you feel courage is beyond your ability. You cannot imagine yourself overcoming the fear and doubt. Courage is a choice. God will strengthen you if you make the choice to obey.

Step into courage

King David prayed for courage (1 Samuel 30). He and his army returned to Ziklag to find it burned to the ground by the Amalekites and their wives and children taken captive. It is easy to point the finger of blame at a time like this, especially at leadership. The men spoke of stoning David.

They were *dis*-couraged. The word means to be separated from courage or to have courage removed from you. We have all experienced the feeling of hope being sucked out of us like a deflating balloon. The bible says the men wept until they had no more power to weep.

And David was greatly distressed; for the people spoke of stoning him, because the soul of all the people was grieved, every man for his sons and for his daughters: but David encouraged himself in the LORD his God. 1 Samuel 30:6 KJV

David *en*-couraged himself in the Lord. He connected with courage or stepped into courage. The Hebrew root word is to seize, catch or cleave. We have the picture of David grabbing on to courage in desperation. You can imagine him getting in his tent and crying out to God for strength. He does not blame God for the circumstance. He does not avoid the battle ahead. He prays for strength. This is required of a leader. Note that none of his army had made a move toward recovering what had been lost. It was David's leadership that caused the men to snap out of their despair and spring into action.

There will be times when we are overwhelmed by circumstance; times when the odds seem so lopsided against us that we feel hopeless. We must have the ability to encourage ourselves in God. Instead of blame or self-pity, we must pray for courage and strength. We know that God helped David in this circumstance and he recovered all. We must also know that God will help us. Stepping into courage is a choice.

Pray for boldness

The disciples prayed for courage and boldness (Acts 4). Peter and John were arrested and made to answer to the religious council for healing a crippled man and causing a commotion by preaching. When questioned about the miracle, they clearly stated that the power and authority was in Jesus Christ.

Now when they saw the boldness of Peter and John, and perceived that they were uneducated, common men, they were astonished. And they recognized that they had been with Jesus. Acts 4:13 ESV

I love this verse of scripture. Being with Jesus had not made them timid or weak. The opposite was true. They were bold and confident in their faith and declared it openly. The religious leaders recognized that this was a result of having "been with Jesus." Peter and John were threatened and commanded to no longer speak or teach in the name of Jesus.

But Peter and John answered them, "Whether it is right in the sight of God to listen to you rather than to God, you must judge, for we cannot but speak of what we have seen and heard."Acts 4:19-20 ESV

Backing down and crawling into a corner to hide was not an option. Obedience to God's call was paramount. Peter and John returned to the gathering of all the new believers and related what happened. Their reaction to this event would be critical to the beginning New Testament church. Can you imagine the results of them giving an evil report like the spies who went into the promise land? The strategy of the enemy was to intimidate them. I am sure there were those present who were completely afraid and wanted to retreat. Leadership requires courage. They prayed with the assembly, not that the persecution would go away, but that they would have boldness to preach in spite of the opposition. It was not a prayer of complaint, "Lord, why is this happening? It's not fair!" It was a prayer for courage and strength.

And now, Lord, look upon their threats and grant to your servants to continue to speak your word with all boldness, while you stretch out your hand to heal, and signs and wonders are performed through the name of your holy servant Jesus." And when they had prayed, the place in which they were gathered together was shaken, and they were all filled with the

Holy Spirit and continued to speak the word of God with boldness. Acts 4:29-31 ESV

God gives strength and courage to do what He has called us to do. This is part of the ministry of the Holy Spirit. Before Pentecost, the disciples were hiding in an upper room. After being filled with the Holy Ghost, we find them preaching on the street corners of Jerusalem. The fruitfulness of the New Testament church would have never been a reality had they remained timid. The old saying is true, "When your knees are knocking, it always helps to kneel on them."

Fight or flight is a choice. On occasion, of course, running is the best option. However, you cannot run from doing what is right. If God has called you, he will give you the strength necessary to do it. If God has given you talents and ability, which He has, know that there is a purpose and a reason. You cannot run from doing what God has called you to do. Just ask Jonah about that one (Jonah 1:1-17).

Metamorphosis

Men gathered themselves around David and they became his army. These were not the cream of the crop, so to speak, but more or less a band of undisciplined rebels.

And everyone who was in distress, and everyone who was in debt, and everyone who was bitter in soul, gathered to him. And he became captain over them. And there were with him about four hundred men. 1 Samuel 22:2 ESV

The men of David's army were not what you would call men of valor. Yet, God worked in them to become what 2 Samuel 23 refers to as "mighty." These were men who stood their ground when others retreated; who risked their lives in service to God and David. By enlisting in God's army, they became men of courage.

God often chooses the weak, untalented and timid to do great exploits. We would look for the big and brave, but God is more concerned with willingness than ability. He is in the business of transformation. Gideon, Moses, David, and many other Bible heroes did not start out that way. The disciples were fishermen and tax collectors, but Jesus made them apostles. God raised them up to be courageous leaders.

God has called you and I to enlist in his service. Perhaps you do not view yourself as the brave soldier type. Regardless, there is a battle raging. We have an enemy opposing us. God has equipped us with weapons and armor and called us to fight the good fight.

For we do not wrestle against flesh and blood, but against the rulers, against the authorities, against the cosmic powers over this present darkness, against the spiritual forces of evil in the heavenly places. Ephesians 6:12 ESV

For the weapons of our warfare are not of the flesh but have divine power to destroy strongholds. We destroy arguments and every lofty opinion raised against the knowledge of God, and take every thought captive to obey Christ 2 Corinthians 10:4-5 ESV

God is able to give you strength and courage. I would venture to guess that God has already worked these things in your character more than you know. We must stop focusing on what we are not in ourselves and start standing on what God says we are in him. In him, we are more than conquerors. In him, we can do all things. In him, our weakness turns to strength. The Lord is our banner. This was the revelation of God's character revealed to Moses when they fought against Amalek (Exodus 17). He is our fortress, our strong tower, our shield, and our source. The battle belongs to the Lord. We must stand on his word and claim his promise.

This is called faith.

PART 3 - FAITH

Now faith is the substance of things hoped for, the evidence of things not seen. Hebrews 11:1 KJV

Faith is an action word. James says, "Faith without works is dead" (James 2:17). It is not a passive feeling; faith motivates us to do something. We tend to think of faith as an overpowering emotion. However, like courage, faith is a choice to believe in something regardless of what circumstance is telling you. It is the choice to stand on something even when your five senses are screaming at you to do otherwise. It is the choice to hope in something outside of yourself. Faith takes courage and courage relies on faith. Both are available to anyone, they are gifts from God for the asking. How do you know when you have received? You do not know until you try. It is called "the step of faith" for that very reason. The act of trying is evidence of faith.

Albert Einstein said in essence, "Nothing happens until something moves." **1.** He was referring to a law of physics, but it also applies to all of life. The person who is fruitful in life is the one who takes initiative. You have to plant a seed in order to one day reap a harvest. The ground does not automatically give fruit just because you want it. Fruitfulness does not come necessarily to those who need it. Jim Rohn said it this way, "The ground says bring me your seed, not your need." **2.** Nature only responds to those who take initiative and plant the seed. You can whine about that and call it unfair, march in the streets and protest, but the laws of nature will not change. Planting seed is a step of faith. The farmer cannot make things grow, that comes from God. But, by faith, he tills the ground, plants the seed and waters. God gives the increase. A lot of time and effort comes in between the sowing of a seed and the reaping of the fruit. Many give up before harvest season. You have to keep the faith.

God helps the helpless, fatherless and widow. God is full of mercy and miracle working power. God has promised provision despite nature, economy or any other obstacles we face. Faith is standing on his word and promise when it is all we have to stand on. Faith is obedience to his word when the situation looks hopeless.

In the book of Matthew, the disciples are in a boat on the sea during a bad storm. Jesus comes walking on the water and the disciples scream because they think it must be a ghost. Jesus tells them not to be afraid and identifies himself. Then Peter comes out of left field and requests to join Jesus on the water. Jesus says, "Come" (Matthew 22:29). So, Peter walks on the water, which we all know is impossible. It is one thing if Jesus walks on the water, we can all accept that, but Peter should not be out there. Peter took initiative. He took the step of faith. He is not really walking on water as much as he is standing on the word Jesus spoke to him. As soon as he looks at the waves, he becomes apprehensive and begins to sink. This happens to us as well when we focus more on circumstance than we do His promise. I am sure the other disciples mocked Peter for sinking. It is easy to criticize when you are a spectator on the sidelines.

Here is the truth: you and I will never walk on the water as long as we remain in the boat. Walking on water defies all natural law and common sense. The disciples focused on the waves, the wind and the dorsal fins. Peter focused on Jesus and His word.

When we focus on what we fear, those things tend to grow and multiply. The twelve spies bring the report back from the promise land, "we were like grasshoppers in their sight and in our sight as well (Numbers 13:33)." Fear has really blown things out of proportion in their minds. They are feeling like tiny little grasshoppers in the face of their enemies.

The problem is, when you feel like a grasshopper you will act like a grasshopper. These insects are not designed to rise up and overcome obstacles like you and I. You never see one of these little guys put up his dukes and start throwing blows. No, they defend themselves by hopping away. Unfortunately, many people do the same thing. They get stirred up to do this or try that, but the first sign of trouble and they hop away. Jesus described this as a person who has no root in themselves (Matthew 13:20-21). They receive the seed with gladness and begin to grow, but when opposition comes, they wither and die.

Grasshoppers are also very good at blending in to their environment. People use this defense mechanism as well. They fear that taking bold steps of faith will make them stand out. They do not want to draw attention to themselves, therefore, they do what everybody else is doing and blend in to the crowd. Peter denied Jesus three times for this reason (Matthew 26:69-75). It is one thing to stand in faith while surrounded by your brethren, and quite another when you are all alone. God created us to have dominion, but our fallen nature has been robbed of the confidence necessary. Faith is putting our confidence in

God's word and his ability to work through us.

That the sharing of your faith may become effective by the acknowledgment of every good thing which is in you in Christ Jesus. Philemon 1:6 NKJV

Fear and faith are opposites. Henry Emerson Fosdick has said: "Fear imprisons, faith liberates; fear paralyzes, faith empowers; fear disheartens, faith encourages; fear sickens, faith heals; fear makes useless, faith makes serviceable; and, most of all, fear puts hopelessness at the heart of life, while faith rejoices in its God." **3.**

Faith says, "I am not a grasshopper, I am a giant killer." Fear is overcome when we focus more on God than on what we see or feel. God has not given us the spirit of fear. Jesus has overcome the enemy. Resist the devil and he will flee from you. You must walk in the Spirit of power, love and a sound mind.

Meekness

This is where the real meaning of meekness comes in. Meek is not weak or timid. Meek is not fighting the battles of life in your own strength or relying on your own talents. Meekness is following God's path for your life and using God's battle plan by faith. It is recognizing our own weakness and shortcomings and relying on his strength to overcome.

Gideon was meek. When God comes to call, he is hiding from his enemies (Judges 6). The angel announces, "You mighty man a valor." It is almost comical. Gideon is wondering who the angel is talking about, "Who me?" The angel explains the mission God has for Gideon, but Gideon is leery.

Eventually, Gideon is convinced by putting out a fleece. You and I need to be convinced we have God with us in our endeavors. He promised he would never leave you nor forsake you. Gideon puts together an army to fight and God shrinks it to three hundred men. The battle plan that God gives does not even include weapons. It seems crazy! He tells them to light candles and hide them inside clay pots to cover the light. When they had surrounded the camp of the Midianites, they broke the clay pots, exposing the light, blew trumpets and shouted, "The sword of the Lord and Gideon is upon you." The enemy defeated itself by turning on each other.

We see Gideon took the initiative by responding to God's voice in faith. He does not rely on human ingenuity or lean on his own understanding. I am sure he was scared to death. Nevertheless, he put his trust in God's call, obeyed God's plan and went forth in courage, relying on God's strength. This is meekness.

What is God calling you to do? It might be something outside of your comfort zone. Have you ever thought it interesting that Paul, the religious zealot, was called to go to the Gentiles as a missionary and Peter, the fisherman, was the apostle to the Jews? We would never have made that executive decision. The resumes would clearly have pointed out these men should be doing just the opposite. God does not want us to trust solely in our own talents and abilities. Paul said, "When I am weak I am made strong" (2 Corinthians 12:10). Our trust should be in Him. This is a scary prospect to our human logic.

...and my speech and my message were not in plausible words of wisdom, but in demonstration of the Spirit and of power, that your faith might not

rest in the wisdom of men but in the power of God. 1 Corinthians 2:4-5 ESV

Nehemiah

The story of Nehemiah rebuilding the wall around Jerusalem is so parallel to life. He arrives in town with the backing of the King, a promise of provision, and lots of enthusiasm. The speech he gives to the residents inspires them to action. They start building with fervor, until the inevitable. The leaders of the region do not like the fact that good is happening to somebody besides themselves and become envious. Sound familiar? Opposition, doubters, critics, and complainers are as old as time.

They first try and discourage the building through ridicule and mocking. A fear of failure is often fueled by a fear of what people will think of you if you fail. Nobody likes being made fun of, looked down upon or hated. You have to decide that your desire to accomplish is greater than your fear of public perception.

For they all were trying to make us afraid, saying, "Their hands will be weakened in the work, and it will not be done." Nehemiah 5:9 NKJV

Intimidation was next on the list of strategies. The wall builders all have families to consider. Nobody wants to put the safety of his family in jeopardy. When the threat of attack came, it would have been natural for them to back down for the sake of their loved ones. The irony here is that the wall they were building would bring security to their families.

And I looked and arose and said to the nobles and to the officials and to the rest of the people, "Do not be afraid of them. Remember the Lord, who is great and awesome, and fight for your brothers, your sons, your daughters, your wives, and your homes." Nehemiah 4:14 ESV

Nehemiah implemented a work and fight policy. While half of the people worked, the others stood guard with weapons, ready to fight. The workers also had weapons ready at hand in case of attack. There will be opposition and obstacles to whatever we try to accomplish for God. Understanding this is half the battle. We must be prepared to stand in faith.

When the mocking and intimidation did not discourage Nehemiah, the accusations began. Stories were spread about the motives behind building the wall. Have you ever had your motives questioned? Because you are trying to accomplish something, people whisper, "He thinks he is better than us!" False accusation is a painful personal attack. They said of Jesus that he was doing miracles by the power of the devil. Jesus told his disciples that they too would endure lies and accusation. It is disheartening.

Nehemiah is accused of setting the stage for his own kingdom. They threaten, "We are going to tell the King." It sounds like schoolyard stuff. Instead of allowing fear of what the King will think, he recognizes the strategy and keeps on building. Good advice! This is a necessary element in leadership. Through false accusation, the enemy wants to draw us away from the work. It is hard to build when you are consumed with defending yourself. Keep building!

It does not end here. The next attempt is interesting. They want Nehemiah to think his life is in danger so he will run, hide, and stop building the wall. Instead of an outright threat, they hire a prophet to pose as a concerned friend. "Let's go hide in the temple because they are coming for you at night."

For this purpose he was hired, that I should be afraid and act in this way and sin, and so they could give me a bad name in order to taunt me. Nehemiah 6:13 ESV

This gives the whole thing a spiritual packaging. However, Nehemiah sees it for what it is. They want him to save his own skin so they can accuse him of selfishness to the people. Nehemiah keeps building through all this and the wall is completed.

In life, you will have to keep building. Faith is the necessary ingredient for pushing through the obstacles and the opposition to your God given goals. You will serve God by faith or serve the enemy by fear. It is that simple. You must know what you believe and you must be determined to stand on what you believe even when the storm is brewing all around you.

Deposits and withdrawals

We know that the bank will not let you make a withdrawal unless you have made some prior deposits. This elementary truth is sometimes lost on the current culture of credit cards and easy financing. Think of faith for a moment like a savings account. You must put money in to build up an emergency fund. This is in anticipation that one day you will have to make a withdrawal. The problem is, of course, we do not think about needs that will "one day arise," we focus on what we want right now. It takes discipline to prepare for the inevitable budget-breaking event. So what do we do if we have no savings? We go into debt. Now the money that should be going into savings is going to pay off a credit card. The next need to arise puts us further in the hole.

You get the picture. Of course, like money, we need faith everyday. Christianity is a life of faith. However, there are times and circumstances that require an extra withdrawal from the reservoir of faith. What happens to the Christian that has made no deposits?

Joseph gave the interpretation for two dreams that Pharaoh had in one night (Genesis 41). One dream had seven healthy cows eaten by seven skinny cows; the other had seven healthy heads of grain consumed by seven withered looking heads of grain. Joseph explained that there would be seven years of prosperity followed by seven years of famine. He then laid out a sound plan for Pharaoh to follow that would sustain Egypt (and the children of Israel). Here is the simple, biblical strategy: during the good times, set aside something for the bad times coming.

How does this apply to faith? People who eat right and exercise get sick like everybody else, but they rebound quicker. It is true of spiritual health as well. You and I need a daily discipline of prayer, worship and bible reading for spiritual strength. Yet, many God loving Christians only pray and search the scriptures during emergencies. Their faith is insufficient for the storms of life. When the storm came upon the disciples in the boat, they were panic-stricken. Jesus said, "Oh ye of little faith (Matthew 8:26)." A little faith might get you by in the day-to-day stuff, but what about crisis times?

But you, beloved, building yourselves up in your most holy faith and praying in the Holy Spirit, keep yourselves in the love of God, waiting for the mercy of our Lord Jesus Christ that leads to eternal life. Jude 1:20-21 ESV

Two words stand out in these verses. The word *build* gives the picture of construction. If you have ever worked in building or observed a construction site, you know there is lots of activity involved. From day to day, it might not seem like much is accomplished. The progress is very methodical. Daily Christian disciplines may not sound exciting, but this is the brick and mortar of faith. The word *keep* comes from a military term and simply means to maintain.

Christianity is not a list of rules and regulations to follow. It is not something we do on Sunday. It is a relationship. Like any relationship, the more time is invested, the more trust is developed. Trust is the issue with faith. Do you trust Him? Do you believe He is in control? Do you believe He has your best interest in mind? Do you trust Him in the areas of future, family and finances? It is easy to say "yes" to all of these in the good times. Do you trust Him in the time of trial and temptation?

Therefore take up the whole armor of God, that you may be able to withstand in the evil day, and having done all, to stand firm. Ephesians 6:13 ESV

The point here is, we need to be prepared for the *evil day* when it comes; the day of assault against our hope in Christ and our trust in His word; the day of weakness and fatigue. If you and I are going to be ready for whatever life throws our way, we must be in constant training. That means time on our knees and in worship. It means time reading his Word and claiming his promises. The Bible says that faith comes by hearing, and hearing by the Word of God (Romans 10:17). His Word is alive and powerful. Jesus said that one of the ministries of the Holy Spirit would be to "bring to your remembrance all things that I said to you (John 14:26)." We need to have put something in the storage tank for the Holy Spirit to draw from.

But he who looks into the perfect law of liberty and continues in it, and is not a forgetful hearer but a doer of the work, this one will be blessed in what he does. James 1:25 NKJV

Not only should we read His word every day, it is also helpful to have a personal creed we go over often, even daily. A creed is simply a statement of belief; a list of some promises that you claim in prayer. These could be truths about God's provision, his strength and help, or his power to work through you. It is important to declare who God is and who you are in God (Psalms 92:2). Unfortunately, creeds such as the Apostles or Nicene Creed have become repeated words without much thought. However, a personal creed is about reinforcing God's word in your own heart. I am not suggesting a formula that is "guaranteed to make you a spiritual giant in 30 days or less." It is important, however, to keep your sword sharp and your faith strong (Ephesians 6:16-17). A sample prayer could be something like this:

Thank You Jesus for forgiveness and grace. You have given me all things pertaining to life and godliness. This includes the strength to endure any trial or temptation that will come my way. Without You I can do nothing. You are the Vine and I am a branch. If I abide in You I can be fruitful. I can do all things through Christ who strengthens me. Nothing is too hard for You. All things are possible for those who believe. I believe You are able to do exceedingly, abundantly beyond anything I can ask, think, or imagine. Greater is He who is in me than he that is in the world. Surely, goodness and mercy shall follow me and You will never leave me nor forsake me. You have taken my feet from the miry clay and put them on a solid rock. I thank You! You have allowed me to escape the corruption that is in the world. You are my refuge and my strength and I trust in You. You are my provider and I depend on You. The battles I face today belong to You. You are the banner and covering over my life, family and finances. Only You have the power to save, heal and deliver. I worship You!

Of course, there is more to prayer than repeating a mantra. This is simply one faith building aspect of standing on God's word in prayer. For a list of scriptures you could incorporate, please see APPENDIX 1.

Do you believe this?

Lazarus had been dead four days when Jesus arrived. His two sisters were disappointed that He had not arrived in time to save their brother's life. We fail to understand that God has a bigger picture in mind. He sees the end from the beginning. We are disappointed in the present circumstance perhaps, but should know that God always has a plan. Each piece of the puzzle fits somewhere and we need to trust him with our future.

Jesus tells Martha that Lazarus will rise again. Martha believes in the resurrection, but to her it is a vague future event that has no bearing on the present situation. Jesus says to her, "I am the resurrection...Do you believe this (John 11:25-26)?" Moments later, Lazarus was walking out of the tomb alive.

When Jesus is on the scene, all things are possible. Do you believe this? Do you believe that God can help you do the job he has called you to do? Do you believe God has government officials, judges, bosses and decision makers in his hands and can steer them in his direction? Do you believe God can open a door that no man can shut or shut a door that no man can open? Do you believe God has the power to protect you and provide for you and your family?

Jesus first found Peter, James, and John on the beach cleaning their nets after a fruitless night of fishing. Jesus got into Peters boat and used it as a podium to speak to the crowd. After the sermon, he tells Peter to go for one more round of fishing. The catch was so big he had to call James and John to come in their boat to help with all the fish. They knew this was nothing short of Jesus working a miracle.

Jesus then says to them, "Follow me and I will make you fishers of men." Before he called them, he demonstrated his concern for their need and his ability to meet that need. If God calls you to do something, then he will provide what is necessary to accomplish the task. Do you believe this?

Let the children come

Jesus said, "Let the children come to me (Matthew 19:14)." My daughter was five years old when we moved to Africa. She attended first through fifth grade in a foreign school. She learned the metric system, a strange way of doing division problems, English with words spelled differently than we spell them and nothing of U.S. history or geography. We tried to fill in the gaps, but feared she would be behind in her education when we returned home. In reality, when enrolled in a U.S.

school, she was way ahead of her class. She was not deprived by not having a TV on the mission field. On the contrary, she was the best reader in her class. While her class talks about foreign countries and different cultures and languages, she has seen it first hand. Will she ever use the Zulu words she learned in Africa? Probably not, but talk about an education.

Your children are not a valid reason to avoid doing what God has called you to do. In fact, we should do God's will for the sake of our children!

I visited a missionary in Zambia who was the Pastor of a church in a little farming community a few hours from the capital city of Lusaka. I went with his family and people from his church to a neighboring fishing village on the Kafue River. There was maybe eight hundred people living there in mud huts with no electricity or running water. The only reason you could tell you were in modern times was the hand me down NBA t-shirts that people were wearing. They fished the river using hand carved boats and homemade nets. We had no problem gathering a crowd to preach to in this village.

This missionary couple had three teenage daughters as pale-skinned as you can imagine. As we were in this village, they were mingling with folks, holding babies, smiling and laughing like this is completely normal. Observing them, I was thinking to myself that most teenage girls are worried about clothes, makeup, hairstyles, and boys. Will these girls be emotionally scarred for life? No way! The oldest had just been accepted to a University in America on a full scholarship.

Doing God's will gives your children an advantage! Hiding from God's call because of fear for your family only sets the stage for your kids to grow up and do the same. It teaches them that selfish agendas are priority over God's purposes. Kids are not dumb. They see through your excuses and are aware that you are running from what you are supposed to be doing.

Our legacy will be fear or faith. The safest place for our families is in the will of God. Peter was safer standing on the water with Jesus than were the disciples who remained in the boat. Jesus said we are to love him more than mother, father, wife, children, or brothers and sisters (Luke 14:26). When we put family first, we are guilty of idolatry. If we will put God first, he will take care of our families (Matthew 6:33).

Steps in overcoming

Confession is the first step towards overcoming. You must admit your fears to the Lord. This sounds simple enough, but it is amazing how we will call our hesitancy everything but fear. We are masters at making excuse and justifying why we cannot move forward or accomplish what we want.

Any of the disciples could have gotten out of the boat and walked on the water with Peter. You know what was going through their minds because it has gone through yours: "Well, Jesus did not call me. He clearly said that to Peter and not to me. If I get out of the boat, it would be the sin of presumption. Besides, the others will think I am just trying to kiss up to Jesus. I do not want to appear to be exalting myself." As the dialog in the mind goes on and on, the opportunity is passing.

You must call it what it is. We will not make the necessary changes until we come to grips with the truth about who we are and the choices we are making. Fear has kept you from doing what God has called you to do long enough. We must stop making excuses and reasoning within ourselves.

The second thing we must do is commit our fears to the

Lord. This also sounds like it should be simple, but this goes cross grain to our nature. We tend to hold things in, carry our own load, lean on our own ability. All you have to do is look at sales figures on sleeping pills, pain medicine, and anti-inflammatory drugs to know our society is stressed out. Fear, of course, is just one of the things robbing us of peace of mind, but it is a major part of the issue. How do you commit this to God? After you identify it, you hand it over in prayer. It has to be a daily prayer of surrender and repentance. You must turn from allowing fear to hold you back from obedience.

I sought the LORD, and He heard me, and delivered me from all my fears. Psalms 34:4 NKJV

Cast your burden on the LORD, and He shall sustain you... Psalms 55:22 NKJV

Cast your cares on Him because He cares for you... 1 Peter 5:7 NKJV

The third step in overcoming is taking up the shield of faith. What happens in between reading this and putting it into action? Things happen; little things that try to talk you out of being bold and stepping out on faith. Ephesians 6 says you must take up the shield of faith so you can extinguish the fiery darts that come against your mind and heart. These arrows aim to inflame your emotions of fear and doubt. You must make a decision that you will not retreat, but will stand firm on His promise. Your reaction to life is your choice. Your attitude marching forward is your choice.

Faith Overcomes Fear

Years before answering the call to go to Africa, I had the opportunity to preach a revival in Kingston, Jamaica. I took my wife and a few people from the church where I was the pastor in Houston, TX. My daughter was two years old at the time and stayed in the U.S. with a babysitter.

It is nearly impossible not to be moved by the need in a third world environment. That week, we saw many come to Christ. On the first night we were there, we preached in an open square, ironically called Nelson Mandela Park, and saw large crowds gather to hear the word and to receive prayer. Many of these attended the meetings during the week at the church. In addition, a number of schools invited us to preach in morning assemblies and pray for the students. You cannot do that in America! We were stirred with perhaps answering the call to a place like this.

On the last day we were to be in Kingston, we went with the local missionary and his wife to look at a house a couple of girls from his church were considering renting. It was located deep in a neighborhood with narrow streets and little homes squeezed in close together. The missionary pastor went into the house with the girls to negotiate with the landlord on their behalf. The missionary's wife was standing next to their car in the driveway. My wife and I crossed the street to stand in the shade behind a little panel van to get some relief from the tropical heat.

We began to have a conversation about being missionaries. "We could do this. We could come here, even to this city and start a church. God would help us." In the middle of this conversation, we heard the pastor's wife scream. From where I stood behind the van, I could not see that five men with machetes had come to mug us.

You never know how you are going to react in that situation. Most men picture themselves punching the person, perhaps giving him a Karate chop or some kind of Rambo heroism. One guy came around the end of the van to where we were standing. I am not sure why I reacted this way, perhaps because I am from Texas, but I head butted him in the chest like a bull and he went falling backwards on the pavement.

I came around the van on the curbside to cross the street, thinking my wife was right behind me. I had not seen that there was a second man who had stepped over the one I knocked down and came at her. She fell back on the ground in terror, and as the guy hovered over her with the knife, handed over her little passport pouch that was hanging around her neck. He took it and began to run. When she screamed, "He has my purse," I had just made it across the street and realized she was not behind me. The man and his partner went running by me.

By this time, the other three men had cut the waist pack off the missionary's wife and went running down the street as well. I gave chase for about the length of two houses when I decided it was not a good idea for me to run after these five machete-carrying thugs into their neighborhood. The whole event took about seven seconds. It was over before the group could even come out of the house to see what was going on.

The fear during those seven seconds is not the issue I tell you about here. Things like that happen so fast you do not have time to feel anything. It was the fear that settled over my life afterwards. Thoughts swirled around in my head: What could have happened? What if I had been murdered and now my widowed wife would raise our daughter alone? What if my wife had been murdered? What if we had both been killed and my daughter would be an orphan? What if my wife had been raped and had to live with that trauma? I had brought her here. I was the one that had said to her, "Let's go on a mission trip." The weight of that was heavy on me. What right did I have to take my family into a dangerous situation? What kind of husband, what kind of father would risk the lives of those he was supposed to be protecting and providing for?

That night at church, the congregation was apologetic for what happened to us in their city. They said for us not to stay away in the future because of this. In truth, this sort of thing happened in Houston, but the gang would have had guns instead of machetes. I told them this and laughed it off.

Upon returning home, I told people the same thing and acted as if it was no big deal. However, inside I was tormented. I would tell people of the conversation we were having when the event took place and then laughingly say, "I guess God closed the door." In reality, it was I closing the door. For the next couple of years, I pushed aside all of God's dealings about the mission field because of fear. The enemy had planted a seed of fear in my heart to prevent future blessing.

Jesus told the parable of a man whom sowed seed on good ground, but the weeds grew up in the field and prevented fruitfulness. Jesus explained this to be the cares of this world that choke out God's word in our lives (Matthew 13:22). Fear is one of those weeds! It is the fear of sacrifice and going without. It is the fear of leaving the familiar and venturing out into the unknown. The fear of discomfort in a world that preaches life is all about being comfortable.

Should we forget all about world evangelism because there is danger out there? Did the New Testament Christians shrink back from opposition and persecution for personal safety? Just the opposite, they prayed for more boldness. Paul often solicited prayer for himself in his letters to the churches for more strength to preach in the face of opposition. The spirit of fear wants to dethrone Christ as our Lord. The goal of the enemy is the same as in the days of Nehemiah: to stop the work.

Faith overcomes fear! It is the choice to believe God. Jesus knew that fear would be an issue in the lives of his disciples. Jesus gave them promises to stand on during times of fear, doubt, and worry. He told them that he would never leave them nor forsake them. In the world, they would have trouble, but he had overcome the world. Do not be worried about where you will sleep, what you will eat, and what will you wear. God clothes the lilies of the field and feeds the sparrows. We are more important than these things and therefore God will surely provide for us. Put the Kingdom of God first and he will take care of all these things.

Does this mean we should skip work and bow out of taking responsibility for our lives? Of course not! It is a promise of supernatural provision and intervention in our lives when we are committed to him and doing his work.

Stepping out

Fear was keeping me from doing what God had called me to do. At a bible conference in Tucson, AZ, I came to a place of repentance and made myself available to God. I felt like Abraham, called to go without knowing exactly where (Hebrews 11:8). I had Africa on my heart, however, did not have a specific place in mind.

Of course, planning and preparation is necessary, but there comes a time for action. Fear always wants to prolong the discussion phase and delay taking the step of faith. When God says, "Go," it is time to go.

Another missionary had told us of a city called Walvis
Bay in the nation of Namibia, and so we made the commitment
to go. I call this, "Africa for beginners." It is a little tourist town
with a fishing industry on the Atlantic coast. Surrounded by
miles and miles of sand dunes, it has to be the biggest beach in
the world. Looking back now, I see that God was allowing us to
get our feet wet. This had been under Apartheid control at one
point, so we got a baptism into the separatist culture. We
learned how to drive on the wrong side of the road and got use
to living without Mexican food. During the time waiting for our
work permits, we traveled to Victoria Falls in Zimbabwe,
Botswana, Cape Town in South Africa, and quite a few game
parks in between. We fell in love with Africa and were gripped
with the need.

After six months, our work permits were rejected in
Namibia. At this point the feeling that we had totally missed
God crept over us. Somewhat unwillingly, we went to
Johannesburg to "scope out the land." The very weekend we
were there to "look," the missionary who had started the work
in SOWETO just seven months earlier had to leave the country
because of his own permit problems. I was asked to come and
baby-sit the church until he could sort things out and return. Of
course, he was not coming back. I did not know that at the time
but God did. God knew if the door opened in SOWETO
before this point, I probably would have been too fearful to
respond. However, I could hardly say "no" under these
circumstances. During the very first church service in
SOWETO, I knew I was supposed to be there. God had called
us to this place.

Why did we go the long way to get there? Why six
months wandering in the wilderness, so to speak? One answer,

God has ways of making us say "yes" to his will. God can help us work through our fears if we are willing. The Holy Spirit is the Comforter.

Another truth, it is easier to guide something that is in motion. When a car is in park, it is difficult to turn the steering wheel. Once you get the vehicle moving, steering becomes quite easy. So it is with our lives. Many people are not doing anything because they are "waiting" for direction. Most often, this is an excuse. God is waiting for movement so he can steer you where he wants you to go. If you wait for all the circumstances to be perfect, you will never do anything. We want a detailed map and plan of action with a guarantee of positive outcome. Life does not work that way. Do something! Nothing happens until something moves. Take the step you know you are supposed to take and God will direct the next step.

I do not know what God has called you to do. Maybe it is the foreign mission field. Perhaps it is the mission field you are living and working in right now. I do know that God has called you to be fruitful. When the Tabernacle was being constructed in the wilderness, the Bible says that God gave the men the wisdom and understanding to know how to build it (Exodus 36:1). God will give you the talent and ability necessary to do His work. He is the vine and we are the branches. If we will abide in him, we will bear much fruit (John 15:4-5).

One more thing about grasshoppers I want you to ponder. Have you ever thought about what a grape or a tomato must look like to a little insect? It must seem like it would be enough to feed the grasshopper and his whole family for weeks. When this bug is on the vine surrounded by all these big, juicy, luscious fruits, it is like an all-you-can-eat buffet. Nevertheless, here is the truth: grasshoppers do not eat fruit. They get right up next to these lovely fruits, turn and eat the leaves!

Do not live your life like a grasshopper. God created you for so much more. Do not settle for second best in your life because of fear or intimidation. Do not let the enemy rob you of the good things God has for you. Say no to fear, rise up in courage and step out in faith toward destiny.

God has called you to fruitfulness!

PART 4 - FRUITFULNESS

So as to walk in a manner worthy of the Lord, fully pleasing to him, bearing fruit in every good work and increasing in the knowledge of God. Colossians 1:10 ESV

Fruitfulness is a miracle that comes from God. The bible says that one plants, one waters, but God gives the increase (1 Corinthians 3:6-7). God created the system in nature of sowing and reaping. Fruitfulness is nature's response to our effort of preparing the soil and planting the seeds. He put Adam in the garden and told him to be fruitful and multiply. We know sin messed up the deal and that barrenness is part of the curse of sin, but fruitfulness is still our desire.

What is fruitfulness? Is this a fancy word for success? Fruitfulness and success are not necessarily synonymous. Most folks would agree that success is not just financial, but that is what comes to mind when we hear the word. I do not subscribe to the doctrine that God has called everybody to be rich. I do believe, however, that God wants us all to be fruitful. Success, for the most part, is tangible. It has to do with what you accumulate and possess. Fruitfulness is mainly intangible. It is about who you are as a person and how your life and character impacts the people around you. Success is temporal. It has to do with what a person accomplishes in this life. Fruitfulness, rather, is a spiritual word; it has to do with what is eternal.

Think about great men of the bible. How did they accomplish the things that they did? Abraham is called the father of those who live by faith. He ventured out from the place he was living in comfort to a land of promise where he lived in tents with his family. He made this choice because he had sights on an eternal promise land (Hebrews 11:9-10).

Moses left the riches of Egypt and chose virtual poverty and struggle. Why? How? His goal was not earthly success, but eternal reward (Hebrews 11:24-26).

The New Testament church was not enamored by this world, but by the next. They sold their possessions and gave to further the gospel message (Acts 4:32-37). They endured persecution and oppression and counted it a privilege to suffer for Christ (Acts 5:41). Paul was consumed by heaven. He said, "For me, to die is gain (Philippians 1:21-24)." This is not some morbid death wish. He is declaring the goal and purpose for which he is living. His hope was beyond this life (1 Corinthians 15:19).

Fruit has to do with what our lives produce for God's glory. Our goals, plans, and labors must be weighed in light of eternity. Of course, we cannot be so heavenly minded that we are no earthly good. However, our priorities should reflect more than temporary pleasure and the accumulation of things that are earth bound. Life is not about inheriting the earth! When Jesus said that the meek would inherit the earth (land), in the mind of the Jewish hearers, they knew he was using the analogy of the promise land to signify God's eternal kingdom and reward

(Matthew 5:5). What a person truly values will be seen in the fruit that they produce. Fear keeps people from fruitfulness because it causes us to focus only on the here and now.

Fruit of repentance

Jesus said that you know a tree by its fruit (Matthew 7:16-17). The Bible describes the fruit of our sinful nature.

Now the works of the flesh are evident, which are: adultery, fornication, uncleanness, lewdness, idolatry, sorcery, hatred, contentions, jealousies, outbursts of wrath, selfish ambitions, dissensions, heresies, envy, murders, drunkenness, revelries, and the like; of which I tell you beforehand, just as I also told you in time past, that those who practice such things will not inherit the kingdom of God. Galatians 5:19-21 NKJV

As Christians, we are to bear fruit in our lives that bring honor to God. Jesus told the woman caught in adultery to go and sin no more (John 8:11). He offered her mercy and not condemnation, unlike her religious accusers. But, this encounter with forgiveness was to produce a change in lifestyle, not a free ticket to keep doing the same old things. It is easy to say you belong to Christ. The world is full of proclaiming Christians. However, if we truly belong to Christ, our lives will produce a recognizable fruit.

But the fruit of the Spirit is love, joy, peace, longsuffering, kindness, goodness, faithfulness, gentleness, self-control. Against such there is no law. Galatians 5:22-24 NKJV

Jesus said we are to follow him and not just believe in him. It is not enough to believe; the Bible says even the devil believes (James 2:19). We must choose to turn from the way we are going and follow Jesus. The word repentance literally means to change one's mind. If you are heading down that wide road that leads to destruction, then you need to hear Jesus calling from the narrow path. You must make a decision to change direction.

John the Baptist said to the religious people of his day that they were to bring forth fruit of repentance. When a person has turned from the sinful nature and chosen to follow Jesus, there is evidence in the fruit of his or her life. Jesus called this being born again (John 3:3). It is a transformation.

Therefore, if anyone is in Christ, he is a new creation; old things have passed away; behold, all things have become new. 2 Corinthians 5:17 NKJV

John the Baptist told people their behavior should change. Stingy people should give. Tax collectors should operate with integrity. Soldiers should be content and not use their position to rip people off (Luke 3:10-14). He addresses each of these in the area of money. Nothing tells the story of our values and priorities like our checkbook registry. Our attitude toward success and material possessions changes when we are truly converted.

When Zacchaeus the tax collector repents, it is evident by the change in his life (Luke 19:1-10). He commits himself to repaying everybody he over taxed in the past. Our lives as Christians should no longer be all about our own survival or prosperity. What makes us feel good or look good should no longer be what motivates us. We have been created for good works in Christ (Ephesians 2:10). We have a new purpose for living, a new creed we live by, and new Lord that we follow. Of course, we have plans, careers, ambitions, and goals. However, these become of lesser importance than our higher calling to fulfill God's plan and purpose for our lives.

Jesus told many parables that deal with fruitfulness. In one parable, the master of the garden comes looking for fruit on a particular tree and finds none. He says to the grounds keeper, "Why is this tree taking up space if it bears no fruit?" *(Luke 13:6-9)* God comes looking for fruit in our lives. Are you bearing fruit? Is your number one desire and goal to bear fruit for His glory?

Let's consider a number of these parables.

The Parable of the Talents (Matthew 25:14-30)

First, God gives opportunity to be fruitful. Many will complain that they have no talent, ability, or avenue to be productive for the Kingdom. God will open doors if you knock; you will find needs to meet if you seek; there are plenty of areas of service if you ask. He comes looking for fruitfulness in what you have been given.

Secondly, fruitfulness is not automatic. The farmer plants seeds on purpose. He prepares the soil, chooses the seed, plants, and then cultivates and waters. If you want to make impact on souls around you, then it must be a goal you set. It must move from the philosophical to the practical. The men in this parable take the talent and go to work. It is not explained how they multiply the master's investment, only that they make the effort.

I heard a story told of two farmers experiencing drought. Both prayed for rain every day. One farmer waited patiently for rain, telling his family that he believed God would provide. The other farmer went out, prepared his field, and planted seed. Which farmer do you think really exhibited faith? Praying for fruitfulness is good and necessary. However, we must put some feet on that prayer and go into all the world and preach the gospel. Jesus did not say pray for revival, he said pray for laborers (Luke 10:2).

The third thing to note in this parable is that God rewards their effort beyond the value of the profit they produced. This is the incredible part. The blessing of God is so far beyond what we can imagine. The glory of heaven so far beyond what we deserve. In real business, the boss-man in the parable would go broke paying out dividends like this. However, God is supernatural and has unlimited resources. Only God can give this kind of yield on investment. He gives the resource to begin with, and then blesses us with a return in this life and in eternity.

As incredible as the deal sounds, the unprofitable servant in the parable still finds room to complain. He actually blames the master for his own unfruitfulness. If we will be honest here, we have to admit there is the ability to make excuse in all of us. This man has justified himself in his mind in order to live with his own conscience. He perhaps knows of the fruitfulness of the other two. But, he reasons that his circumstances are different. He knows he has been called to be fruitful, but "the timing is not quite right."

When the master returns, he cuts through all the excuses and calls the unprofitable servant, "wicked and lazy." This man then confesses the real reason for his barrenness when he admits, "I was afraid." All the other words were just a smoke screen for the real issue. Fear kept him from taking the risk necessary to be fruitful. Fear caused him to procrastinate until the time of opportunity had passed. Fear made survival a priority over productivity. He buried his talent because he was afraid.

How many talents have you buried over the years for the same reason? We are afraid of the commitment necessary to succeed. We fear looking like fools if we fall flat on our face. The voices of self-doubt say we are crazy for even thinking about trying.

Perhaps we fear success itself. Will fruitfulness change me as I have seen it change others? We all know the stories of people who have become successful but lost their family through neglect. They were more consumed with career than the truly valuable things in life. The media loves a story about a high profile person caught in sexual escapades. If the CEO of a company, politician, or especially a preacher, is caught in a scandal, it is front-page news. We reason, "This is what happens to people who succeed. It is a long way down from the top. Who are we to survive success?" Therefore, we put on the cloak of false humility and bury our talent.

The master did not consider this a valid excuse. He expected a return on investment in spite of fears and doubts present in all three of these men.

Jesus is the Vine (John 15:1-8)

Jesus said that he is vine and we are the branches. A branch cannot bear fruit unless attached to the vine. In the same way, we can do nothing apart from him. "If we abide in him," Jesus said, "we will bear much fruit." To abide means dependence and obedience. We cannot do it our way and expect his fruit. We cannot do it on our own and expect the miracle of fruit. Jesus uses this law of nature to paint a very clear picture.

Fruitfulness brings glory to the father. Think about your own children and the pride you feel with their accomplishments. Parents love to brag about their children. When they succeed, we think it validates our parental skills. Surly, we passed on the gene that caused them to be so wonderful.

How much more is our heavenly Father pleased with our victories and successes? He created us to be productive. He gave us the talent and ability necessary. All good things come from him, including the opportunities that life presents us.

How do you feel when your children hold back from doing what you know they could? As parents, we desire to give our children all the tools necessary to succeed in life. But, we cannot do it for them. They each have their own choices to make with what is given to them.

I do not know all that God has given you. It is easy to focus on the negatives in life and make excuse for not being fruitful. It is easy to compare your lot in life to others and feel that life is not fair. Dwelling on the road of "if only…" will cause you to stagnate. If we abide in him, he promises much fruit. He does not qualify this by talking about soil conditions, weather, or region. Regardless of circumstance both past and present, if you abide in him you will be fruitful. That is his promise to you and me.

The Pearl of Great Price (Matthew 13:45-46)

Jesus told a parable of a man who found a pearl of great price.

He went and sold everything he had to raise the funds so he could purchase that pearl.

First, think of yourself as the pearl. Maybe you do not feel like you are worth very much. All your life, perhaps, you have been told you will not accomplish anything. Every time you have tried to shine, you ended up stinking instead. The market place determines the value of an item. The seller can put a price tag on something, but if people are unwilling to pay the price, it is not as valuable as he thinks. He then lowers the price until somebody buys it. Maybe you feel like you have little worth because people have not placed much value on you. Rejection, betrayal, and neglect, all leave a person feeling worthless.

Jesus is the pearl merchant. This merchant knows his pearls and when he sees this one, he has to have it. He goes and sells everything in order to purchase this pearl for himself. That is how much Jesus values you. In essence, a pearl is just a hardened teardrop. When a piece of dirt gets inside its shell, an oyster produces a tear like substance to stop the irritation. As this hardens around the dirt, a pearl forms. The value is not in the pearl itself, but in what a person is willing to pay for it. The buyer sets the value.

Jesus gave his life to redeem you from the curse of sin. He values you so much that he was willing to pay the ultimate price. We belong to him.

But God demonstrates His own love toward us, in that while we were still sinners, Christ died for us. Romans 5:8 NKJV

Self worth in this world is tied to how you look, how much you have or how much you accomplish. In South Africa, I ministered to people who had been told all their lives that they were fourth-class citizens because of the color of their skin. This world's value system is wrong! You are valuable because you are a human soul created by a God who loves you. The world may not value you because of what you are, but God sees what you can become. Life is not about what you can accomplish, but what he can accomplish through you.

I can do all things through Christ who strengthens me. Philippians 4:13 NKJV

Secondly, see yourself as the merchant. The buyer in this parable has seen many pearls in his time and knows the market. This pearl is large, perfectly round with spectacular color and beauty. He has to have it! He knows this is the opportunity of a lifetime. He must move quickly before somebody else buys it. We have all experienced that kind of desire, but this man is willing to sell everything to purchase the pearl.

Think about this. Buying this pearl is not a very wise financial move. I am sure his associates in the pearl business tried to talk him out of it. You cannot tie up all your capitol in one investment. You need to spread it out a little. What if the bottom falls out of the pearl business? You cannot eat a pearl. You cannot live in a pearl. However, this man saw something they did not. He was willing to liquidate all his assets so he would have enough to purchase this one pearl of great price.

Jesus is the pearl. We do not have to sell everything to follow Jesus, but everything does become secondary. He is the pearl that is precious above all others. Our lives as Christians are consumed with bringing glory and honor to him. The world thinks we are foolish, but we have found something better than anything this earth offers.

Yes, everything else is worthless when compared with the priceless gain of knowing Christ Jesus my Lord. I have discarded everything else, counting it all as garbage, so that I may have Christ... Philippians 3:8 NLT

One of the first things I had to do when I moved to Africa was purchase a vehicle. Providence arranged an American moving back to the United States who had a vehicle for sale. I was able to make the purchase in U.S. dollars, which worked out for both of us. This man had lived in Africa for three years. Prior to coming, he had owned a business in America that he sold to finance himself to be there. He was now out of money and so he was going back home.

I was impressed with that level of sacrifice and inquired about what sort of work he was involved. Was he working with some sort of Christian mission? Was he involved in a clinic, orphanage, AIDS education, or schooling? NO. This man had sold everything so he could be part of a program whose mission is saving Cheetahs. It turns out the local farmers do not appreciate Cheetahs killing their livestock so are in the habit of shooting them. These poor cats need protection. This man sacrificed three years of his life and all his money to save Cheetahs. The world says, "Wow! That is positive." Give yourself to saving Cheetahs and the world is impressed. However, if we put Jesus and his mission as a priority in our lives, then the world calls us foolish.

People gave me a lot of grief when I made the decision to move to Africa. What is going to happen to your daughter? Where are you going to live? How will all your needs be met? I did not know all the answers. I did know, however, that I had a pearl. Fear causes you to look only at the sacrifice. Love causes you to look at the pearl and faith causes you to trust.

The disciples left their nets behind to follow Jesus (Matthew 4:20). The woman at the well left her water pot and went to tell the towns people about him (John 4:28-29). We all have plans, goals, ambitions, and desires, but we are to put Christ first. People fear surrendering to God's will for their lives because of what they might lose. The devil uses the same lie today he used in the Garden of Eden: God is keeping something from you. We fear going without life's pleasure or comfort.

Truly, truly, I say to you, unless a grain of wheat falls into the earth and dies, it remains alone; but if it dies, it bears much fruit. John 12:24 ESV

Fruitfulness requires that the seed must die. Whatever we do give up or miss out on is small and petty compared to the pearl which we receive. Not everyone is called to go to the mission field, but we are all called to be fruitful where we are. Fruitfulness requires planting yourself by faith.

The third view of this parable is from the eye of the vendor. Has it ever struck you that somebody is selling this pearl? Who is this person? Perhaps he was a merchant that discovered this pearl in the market one day and fell in love with it. Why is he selling? Would you sell your pearl? The beauty and perfection of the pearl amazed you at one time and you had to have it. Maybe you went and sold all that you had to be able to buy the pearl. Despite advice to the contrary, you felt it was worth the investment, the opportunity of a lifetime. You acquired the pearl because you saw something others did not.

Now, somebody is offering a large sum of money. Should you sell? You put your hand to the plow of fruitfulness, but other things are now calling you. You have other plans and other priorities. Think of all the excuses and reasoning that must be going through this man's head. The voices of protest before he acquired the pearl are now coming back to him. The pearl has lost its luster in his eyes. He used to brag about the pearl, but now he finds it easy to criticize. After all, there is more to life than one pearl.

Are you willing to sell? Time has a way of making things cloudy. We begin the race strong and full of ambition. The voices from the sidelines are muffled by our focus on the finish line. Determination drives us down the track. However, after awhile, the track seems to grow longer and longer. Our body starts to scream at us to stop, slow down, or take a short cut. The goal gets lost by the pressing need of the moment.

Has this happened to you? Has fruitfulness for God been put on a back burner because of the business of life? If this were a TV game show, "Let's Trade Your Pearl" with host Monty Lucifer, would you play the game? What would make you willing to sell out? Is it the material things of this world that lure you away? Is all the time and effort to pay the payments on all the stuff we want, but do not have time to use, keeping you from fruitfulness? Maybe you have traded the pearl of "great" price for a "smaller and less expensive" version. A fake pearl can look real to everybody, but the owner knows the truth. Have you sold your pearl?

In truth, people do sell, and usually very cheap. Judas sold Jesus into the hands of his enemies for thirty pieces of silver. Paul mentions a disciple named Demus. We do not know much about him, but the fact that he was with Paul says a lot. He was obviously converted. He had a heart for God and for the souls of men. We can imagine that he had seen many miracles. Paul was a great example of sacrifice and labor, prayer and right living. Yet, Demus was drawn away from service with Paul.

Demus has forsaken me having loved this present world and departed to Thessalonica… 2 Timothy 4:10 NKJV

What was it that drew him away? Maybe he wanted a slower pace. Perhaps he did not have the stomach for persecution. It could be that the pearl had lost its luster. Regardless of why, history records this man sold his pearl.

Do not sell your pearl. Calvin Coolidge said, "Nothing in this world can take the place of persistence. Talent will not; nothing is more common than unsuccessful people with talent. Genius will not; unrewarded genius is almost a proverb. Education will not; the world is full of educated derelicts. Persistence and determination alone are omnipotent. The slogan 'press on' has solved and always will solve the problems of the human race." **1.**

Sometimes the voices are loud and the pressure to trade your pearl is great. We have to remember that in Jesus we are rich beyond anything this world could possibly offer. This world will fade away with all its gold, silver, diamonds, and pearls. We have a treasure in heaven. Do you know what they do with gold in heaven? They pave the streets with the stuff. The most sought after substance on earth, and in heaven, it is used as asphalt. Do not sell your pearl!

"Do not lay up for yourselves treasures on earth, where moth and rust destroy and where thieves break in and steal, but lay up for yourselves treasures in heaven, where neither moth nor rust destroys and where thieves

do not break in and steal. For where your treasure is, there your heart will be also. Matthew 6:19-21 ESV

The Sheep and Goats Matthew 25:31-46

This parable is sobering. The fruit that Jesus is looking for is service to others. This is so contrary to the selfish world we live in. This goes cross grain to the philosophy of "look out for number one" that so many live by today. Why are we so selfish? Why are we so consumed with our own wants and needs?

Fear is one factor. We fear going without. Who is going to meet my needs? Who is going to look out for me? Nobody! If we give of ourselves, we fear there will be nothing left for us. We fear what others will think of us as a servant. The person served is more important than the servant. When we are served, it raises our social status. This is why we want servants. This is why the mother of James and John requested of Jesus positions of greatness for her two sons (Matthew 20:20-21). A servant is the lowest of social castes. Nobody aspires to be a servant.

Think of the impact Jesus had on His disciples when He washed their feet (John 13:1-17). Peter is appalled by this and rebukes Jesus. But, Jesus set an example for us to follow. He told his disciples if they wanted to be great in Kingdom of God, they had to become servants (Matthew 20:26).

In this parable of the sheep and the goats, Jesus says, "As you have done to the least of these my brethren, you have done it to me." In our minds, we separate serving Jesus from serving people. However, in light of this parable, how do you serve Jesus without serving people? If we only care about the "rules" of Christianity and forget about the "people," then we become like the Pharisees and religious leaders of Jesus' day.

Jesus said we are to let our light shine so that men will see our good works and glorify God (Matthew 5:16). In our world of selfishness, a kind gesture stands out. Of course, letting your light shine is more than doing good deeds. People must know the "why" behind what you are and what you do. But, nothing makes an impact on people like serving them.

The fruit of the righteous is a tree of life, and he who wins souls is wise. Proverbs 11:30 NKJV

Albert Schweitzer said, "I don't know what your destiny will be, but one thing I do know: the only ones among you who will be really happy are those who have sought and found how to serve." **2.**

For even the Son of Man came not to be served but to serve, and to give his life as a ransom for many." Mark 10:45 ESV

One wish

What if you were granted one wish, what would be your request? Most people on our planet live with only their own interests in mind. They pursue self-gratification without considering how that will affect people around them. Examples of this are all around us. Just look at the number of broken homes. This is especially true when somebody is in a position of power or authority. Human nature is such that we will use that position for personal advantage.

Solomon was king of Israel. As king, he could do just

about anything he wanted. He makes the rules. He could use the power he had to enrich himself. He could use the people to serve him and his interest. Most kings through history have done exactly this. Then on top of all this, God gives Solomon a blank check. He grants Solomon one wish (1 Kings 3:3-14)

What would you do? Be honest. Would you do something noble or something selfish? Would you do something for the good of humanity or something good for yourself? Would you wish for money, long life, power, or revenge?

The truth is we make this choice every day. You and I choose daily whom we are going to serve. Are we mindful of needs around us or only our own? It is a daily choice.

Solomon prays an unselfish prayer. He does not ask for money, long life, power, or revenge. Amazing! He wants to be all that God has called him to be. He wants to be a better person, a better servant. He asks for wisdom from God to be a better king. The one thing that he wishes for above all others is to fulfill the task that God has given him. Solomon wants to be fruitful for God.

More than likely, you are not a king. Yet each of us does have purpose in life. Every seed has fruit producing potential within. We each have talents, opportunities, a job to do, perhaps even a position of authority. These are gifts (Psalms 75:6-7)! We are stewards of the things given to us and must give an account (Luke 12:48). God expects us to do our very best. Regardless of what role you have been called to in life, God has something to say about your performance.

And whatever you do, in word or deed, do everything in the name of the Lord Jesus, giving thanks to God the Father through him. Colossians 3:17 ESV

Wives, submit to your husbands as to the Lord. Husbands, love your wives, just as Christ loved the church and gave himself up for her Children, obey your parents in the Lord, for this is right. Fathers, do not exasperate your children; instead, bring them up in the training and instruction of the Lord. Slaves (or employees), obey your earthly masters with respect and fear, and with sincerity of heart, And masters (or employers), treat your slaves in the same way. Ephesians 5:22-6:9 NIV

So in Christ we who are many form one body, and each member belongs to all the others. We have different gifts, according to the grace given us. If a man's gift is prophesying, let him use it in proportion to his faith. If it is serving, let him serve; if it is teaching, let him teach; if it is encouraging, let him encourage; if it is contributing to the needs of others, let him give generously; if it is leadership, let him govern diligently; if it is showing mercy, let him do it cheerfully. Romans 12:5-8 NIV

Do you feel the weight of your calling? Do you understand the privilege and responsibility you have been entrusted with? Solomon understood this. He knew that God is the one who made him king. This was not an elected position that somehow he could take credit for winning. Solomon was well aware that he was responsible before God.

Solomon also knew the task was bigger than he could accomplish on his own. He needed God's help and wisdom to be a good king. He needed a heart for God's people. Therefore, he prays an unselfish prayer. "God, make me a good king, a good leader, a servant of your people. Give me wisdom so I might fulfill the purpose you have given me. Make me a blessing to your people." Have you ever prayed that prayer?

Have you ever prayed, "God, make me a good husband. Make me a blessing to my wife. Help me not to be a jerk." Have you prayed that? The bible says that a wife is a gift from God. "God, make me a blessing to my children. Help me to be a good father, a good example, a good leader in the home." That is a prayer we need in our society today. Maybe you had none of those things growing up. It is time to break the cycle.

"God, make me a good wife. I want to be a blessing to my husband. Let my words build him up instead of tear him down." Have you prayed that? "God make me a good mother." Maybe you were constantly yelled at or put down as a child. God made motherhood and he can help you if you ask.

"God, make me a blessing to my parents. I don't want to be one of those ungrateful teenagers filled with attitude." Have you prayed that?

"God make me a blessing to my employer; my school; my neighbors."

Have you asked God to make you a good church member? "God, make me a blessing to my pastor. I do not want to be the reason he is getting grey hair. I do not want to be the reason he is considering a career change. God, make me a blessing to my church. I want to be a good example and a source of encouragement." Are you involved in serving at your local church? That would be something to consider in prayer. It is a privilege. "God, make me a good Sunday school teacher; usher; nursery worker." Have you prayed that prayer? "God, make me a blessing to those people that are around me."

If we would be honest, our prayers are generally a little more selfish. We pray, "God, make people treat me better! Lord, I wouldn't be this way if things were different."

We probably think about being blessed a lot more often than being a blessing. We pray, "God, deal with my wife to submit! Why won't she…"

Complaining comes much easier and more natural. We criticize our church rather than pray about how we could be a blessing. People, including you and me, tend to wait for others to change around us before we make our move. Our prayer is, "Gimme, gimme, gimme."

Solomon prays, "Make me a blessing." I believe this prayer could change your whole life. It could change your relationships, your marriage, and your ministry. It is a change of focus.

This change of focus and attitude is actually the key to blessing and fruitfulness. Solomon pleases God with this prayer and he blesses him because of it. Not only does Solomon receive what he prayed for, but all the stuff he didn't ask for: riches, power, and long life. People are consumed with being blessed, yet they are going about it the wrong way. God has no problem blessing us if our hearts are right. We will never be fruitful if we are only concerned about ourselves. Solomon's prayer will change your attitude and perspective.

But seek first his kingdom and his righteousness, and all these things will be given to you as well. Matthew 6:33 NIV

Jesus said, "It is more blessed to give than to receive (Acts 20:35)." How can this be true? Simple. A seed kept to yourself is yours alone, but when you plant a seed, it has the potential to produce fruit. Giving is more productive than receiving. Giving is about being a blessing and not just being blessed. This is the attitude that will yield fruit.

Hannah's prayer

Hannah was barren (1 Sam 1:1-20). In her day, that was considered a reproach. To her, it was an unacceptable condition. Elkanah, her husband, asked her, "Am I not better to you than ten sons?" He did not get it. To make matters worse, he had another wife who was very fruitful. This rival woman would rub Hannah's nose in her barrenness. Hannah was desperate.

The Bible records that every year Elkanah and his family would go to Shiloh and worship. I am sure every year, and all the time in between, Hannah was praying to God for children. Hannah knew from history of Sarah and Rachel to whom God gave children after years of barrenness. She knew that fruitfulness belonged to God.

Have you ever prayed for something for years without apparent answers? Many will give up, lose faith, and surrender to their circumstance. Others will strike out on their own and "make it happen" one way or another. Fruit comes in season. We sow in one season and reap a harvest in another. We must be patient and keep the faith.

Why did it take so long for God to answer the prayer of Hannah? We do not know. The text records only the prayer that was answered.

And she vowed a vow and said, "O LORD of hosts, if you will indeed look on the affliction of your servant and remember me and not forget your servant, but will give to your servant a son, then I will give him to the LORD all the days of his life, and no razor shall touch his head." 1 Samuel 1:11ESV

Other times when she made her request, perhaps, she

was asking only for herself. She wanted fruitfulness for herself. Her desire was to end *her* barrenness, end *her* reproach and stop the mouth of *her* rival. It was all about her. We must ask ourselves the question "Is it all about me?" There is nothing wrong with wanting children, of course. In truth, many of the desires we have in life are not evil. However, God wants to be first in our lives. He wants relationship with us. He wants to be more than our sugar daddy who gives us stuff.

You ask and do not receive, because you ask wrongly, to spend it on your passions. James 4:3 ESV

Hannah's prayer was answered when it was connected to what God wanted. Eli was the priest at this time with his two sons, Hophni and Phinehas, and the need for godly leadership was apparent to her. She vows to release her child to the service of God. She prays for fruit that would glorify God and meet a kingdom need.

Harvest time

While living in Namibia, I had an unruly lemon tree in my back yard that needed pruning. After trimming the branches, I loaded them up to take to the dump. The landfill was five miles or so out into the sand dunes. When I drove up, I was directed to back up to this certain spot. Before I could even get out of my vehicle, people surrounded it. These were not landfill workers, but residents. They were families with small children who lived at the dump and survived off the scraps of others. It was heartbreaking.

The man in charge of the landfill came over with a whip and began to drive the beggars away from the back of the SUV. They began to back off, disappointed that all I had were tree branches. The landfill worker started pulling the trimmings out of the truck and this revealed that quite a few lemons were still in tack. To me, they were just over ripe lemons that served no purpose. To these families, it was a meal for the day. They surged forward and began grabbing the lemons, ignoring the thorns.

We live in a hurting world that needs Jesus. Are you hungry for fruit? Are you desperate like Hannah, tired of barrenness? It is easy to be like the Priest and the Levite in the parable of the Good Samaritan (Luke 10:30-36). We are consumed with our own lives and busy meeting our own needs. The problem is not a lack of compassion, but a blindness that comes from inward focus. A mentality that says, "Somebody else will do it. What I am doing is more important." The priest and the Levite were probably busy doing "religious" things and felt completely justified. If we want to be fruitful for God, we must have a heart for people.

You may say that there are still four months until harvest time. But I tell you to look, and you will see that the fields are ripe and ready to harvest. John 4:35 CEV

Jesus said to look and see the harvest is ripe. First, this implies that our eyes can be somewhere else. Opportunity is all around us, but we will have to look for it. Jesus is focused on the lost. He told his disciples to focus on the lost and to make disciples who would be focused on the lost. Our daily prayer should be for eyes that would see the needs around us.

Second, there is an urgency to the task. Time is limited and we cannot put this off. The sad reality is we can miss opportunity and the harvest can be lost.

We must work the works of him who sent me while it is day; night is coming, when no one can work. John 9:4 ESV

The third truth to consider is labor. Jesus told us we should pray to God for laborers in the harvest (Matthew 9:37-38). We will labor for what is important to us. Each of us has a value system. Our labors, investment, and attitude all reveal what we value. Maybe sports, material possessions, or recreation gets your heart pumping.

Jesus told parables about a lost sheep and a lost coin. These describe the heart of God toward wayward humanity (Luke 15:1-10). The woman sweeps the whole house to find the lost coin. She does not complain about the amount of effort involved, she rejoices over finding her lost treasure. The shepherd does not say, "Ninety nine is good enough." He leaves them to go look for the lost one.

Each of these parables finishes with the statement, "There is joy in heaven over one soul who repents." This tells us the value system of heaven. In a world with billions of people, when just one soul repents, heaven takes notice and celebrates. One human soul is more valuable than all the riches of this world combined (Matthew 16:26). The reward of soul winning outweighs the cost. The joy of fruitfulness is a key motivator.

He who goes out weeping, bearing the seed for sowing, shall come home with shouts of joy, bringing his sheaves with him. Psalms 126:6 ESV

No matter where you are in life, God is looking for fruit. We are to bear fruit that brings glory to God the Father. We are to bear fruit that testifies to the world of God's grace and redemptive power. We are to labor for earth's true treasure, the souls of men. God's word to us is the same from Genesis to Revelation: "Be fruitful and multiply."

"Don't be afraid to go out on a limb. That's where the fruit is."
3. H. Jackson Browne

APPENDIX

Some scriptures you can incorporate in faith building prayer:

The earth and everything on it belong to the LORD. The world and its people belong to him. *Psalms 24:1* CEV

I am the vine; you are the branches. Whoever abides in me and I in him, he it is that bears much fruit, for apart from me you can do nothing. *John 15:5* ESV

I can do all things through Christ who strengthens me. *Philippians 4:13* NKJV

And Jesus said to him, "'If you can'! All things are possible for one who believes." *Mark 9:23* ESV

Ah, Lord GOD! It is you who have made the heavens and the earth by your great power and by your outstretched arm!

Nothing is too hard for you. *Jeremiah 32:17* ESV

His divine power has granted to us all things that pertain to life and godliness...*2 Peter 1:3* ESV

No, in all these things we are more than conquerors through him who loved us. *Romans 8:37* ESV

Surely goodness and mercy shall follow me all the days of my life, and I shall dwell in the house of the LORD forever. *Psalms 23:6* ESV

Now to him who is able to do far more abundantly than all that we ask or think, according to the power at work within us, *Ephesians 3:20* ESV

Little children, you are from God and have overcome them, for he who is in you is greater than he who is in the world. *1 John 4:4* ESV

No temptation has overtaken you that is not common to man. God is faithful, and he will not let you be tempted beyond your ability, but with the temptation he will also provide the way of escape, that you may be able to endure it. *1 Corinthians 10:13* ESV

You shall remember the LORD your God, for it is he who gives you power to get wealth, that he may confirm his covenant that he swore to your fathers, as it is this day. *Deuteronomy 8:18* ESV

And we know that for those who love God all things work together for good, for those who are called according to his purpose. *Romans 8:28* ESV

But thanks be to God, who gives us the victory through our Lord Jesus Christ. 1 Corinthians 15:57 ESV

NOTES

Part 1 Fear

1. Don Colbert, M.D., Deadly Emotions, Nashville, Tennessee, Thomas Nelson, Inc., page 95

2. Rick Warren, The Purpose Driven Life, Grand Rapids, Michigan, Zondervan, page 28-29

3. Lisa Jimenez, M. Ed., Conquer Fear, Mechanicsburg, PA, Executive Books, page 105

4. Lisa Jimenez, M. Ed., Conquer Fear, Mechanicsburg, PA, Executive Books, page 5

5. Peter T. McIntyre, http://www.quoteworld.org/category/confidence/author/peter_t__mcintyre

6. http://acronyms.thefreedictionary.com/False+Evidence+Appearing+Real

7. Edmund Burke, *On the Sublime and Beautiful.* Vol. XXIV, Part 2. The Harvard Classics. New York: P.F. Collier & Son, 1909–14; Bartleby.com, 2001. www.bartleby.com/24/2/

Part 2 Courage

1. George Patton, http://zbh.com/sermons/easy.htm
2. Tom Brokaw, The Greatest Generation, New York, Random House, Inc., page 24

Part 3 Faith

1. Albert Einstein, http://www.squidoo.com/selfhelp30
2. Jim Rohn, excerpts from The Treasury of Quotes, Copyright 1993, 2002 by Jim Rohn International, page 6
3. Henry Emerson Fosdick, The Meaning of Faith, page 195,
    http://books.google.com/books?id=HVYs8kEGhZM
    C&pg=PA195&lpg=PA195&dq=fear+imprisons&sour
    ce=web&ots=VbDw7vm44Q&sig=Y3g8AJG2RmFK0
    NObzdMg4AuPY6Q

Part 4 Fruitfulness

1. Calvin Coolidge, Quotation #2771 from Laura Moncur's Motivational Quotations,
    http://www.quotationspage.com/quote/2771.html
2. Albert Schweitzer, Quotation #4120 from Cole's Quotables,
    http://www.quotationspage.com/quote/4120.html
3. H. Jackson Browne,
    http://www.quoteworld.org/quotes/1971

Scripture References

Scriptures marked as "(CEV)" are taken from the Contemporary English Version © 1995 by American Bible Society.

Scriptures marked MKJV are from the Modern King James Version, copyright © 1962-1998 by Jay P. Green, Sr.

Scriptures marked as ESV are from The Holy Bible, English Standard Version ©2001 Crossway Bibles, a publishing ministry of Good News Publishers.

The Bible text designated (NIV) is from HOLY Bible, NEW INTERNATIONAL VERSION Copyright © 1973, 1978, 1984 by INTERNATIONAL Bible Society

The Bible text designated (NKJV) is from The New King James VERSION, copyright (c) 1982, Thomas Nelson, Inc.

The Bible text designated (KJV) is from The King James Version

ABOUT THE AUTHOR

David J. Drum has over twenty years of ministry experience with the Christian Fellowship Ministries, serving as pastor and international evangelist. He spent five years as a missionary in SOWETO, South Africa. He is the author of three books. David resides with his wife Hilda in Santa Rosa, CA.

For more information visit www.davidjdrum.com

ALSO AVAILABLE FROM YOUR FAVORITE BOOKSTORE:

Twice Dead: The True Death and Life Story of Roman Gutierrez
By David J. Drum
ISBN: 978-0-9856041-0-3
When Roman Gutierrez was eleven years old, his father died from a heroin overdose. Roman resolved, in his anger and his pain, that someday God would take him the same way. He became an addict, a year later he went to juvenile detention for stealing, and attempted suicide the year after that. At fifteen he got into a fight and was pronounced dead for six minutes. At nineteen he was stabbed by his best friend, and pronounced dead for five minutes. When Roman was twenty-five, he shot up all the heroin he had so his torment would end ... and realized he didn't want to die. That's when a miracle occurred... (for more info visit www.TwiceDeadMinistries.com)

Still Taking the Land
By David J. Drum
ISBN: 978-0-9817634-9-1
The Christian Fellowship Ministries (CFM) began as the humble desire of Pastor Wayman Mitchell to put into practice the principles of discipleship, evangelism, and church planting outlined in the Holy Bible. After forty years of obedience to Christ's Great Commission, there are more than 1,800 CFM churches in 125 countries, with an ever-increasing number of new churches being planted each year. This volume presents the practical experience of Pastors Wayman and Greg Mitchell, especially the Biblical principles that have guided CFM growth. Included are essential guidelines of church planting ranging from hands-on application to those of a spiritual nature, as well as a firsthand interview with straight answers to important questions for both those who feel the call of God to enter the ministry and those pastors who are raising up and sending out new workers. For more info visit www.davidjdrum.com)

Offering Stories, Quotes, and Illustrations
Volume 1
By Robert Polaco
ISBN: 978-0-9817634-5-3
Volume 1 is a compilation of over 200 offering stories, quotes, and illustrations. Each illustration also contains a note line where pastors or administrators can indicate the date on which the illustration was used, preventing the potential embarrassment of reusing an illustration. This is a must have companion for any pastor or church administrator.

Offering Stories, Quotes, and Illustrations
Volume 2
By Robert Polaco
ISBN: 978-0-9817634-7-7
Volume 2 is the anticipated sequel in Robert Polaco's compilation series, and includes 375 new entries organized with descriptive titles. This is a must have companion for any pastor or church administrator, filled with illustrations that inspire people to liberality. These illustrations often include supporting scriptural references, and each entry includes a line where one can choose to write in where or when it was used.

Freedom To Choose
By E. L. Kidwell
ISBN: 978-0-9817634-1-5
Visit the Kingdom of Heaven before Earth was created. Enter the throne room of God, and experience the events before time began. Discover the secrets of why hell's chief accuser betrayed the love and perfection of His Creator, and set himself to destroy the race of mankind in seething hatred. Enjoy this thought-provoking drama as it brings to life the Genesis account of the Bible.

Made in the USA
San Bernardino, CA
16 July 2015